CW00499348

Contents

Dedication

This book is dedicated to my children, Michelle, Robert, Vianney and Jamie, and to my incredible grandchildren.

I also want to add a special dedication to George and Gwen Windmill, who I affectionately and lovingly knew as Uncle George and Aunty Gwen, and for their love in my life.

Chapter One

It was another cool summer evening as I sat in my peaceful, glorious garden, smiling contentedly, and watching the fun activity, while those I loved giggled and played away uninhibited.

Oh, how I loved to hear the excitement and joy coming from my young grandson Josh, as he ran around the back garden, screeching with joy as the football zoomed back and forth during the rough and tumble with his uncles, two out of my three sons, Vianney and Jamie.

Breathing in the cool, summer evening air, I gazed upon the lovely fresh green grass, the pear tree, and tropical coloured flowers that stood brilliant in all their splendour. Now and again, Joshie interrupted my thoughts with overjoyed laughing as he yelled through bouts of laughter, 'Grandma, help!'

His Uncles grabbed him playfully as ran around the garden with him on their shoulders.

Yes, life was good today, I thought as I smiled at them all. Looking at Joshua took me back to when my boys were little. Vianney was a good-looking child with his big blue eyes and blond hair, and then there was our Jamie. He was the baby of my four kids.

'The scrapings of my pot,' my Irish Mother use to say. He was so handsome for his years and looked as cute as a button in his little baseball cap.

Oh yes, I am truly blessed, I couldn't help but think as I drifted off into deep thought to memories of a past life that seemed to creep from a corner of my mind. It wasn't unusual for me to drift off into one of my many daydreams, as I sat comfortably and cosy in my back garden. The voices of my family faded into the distance, as pictures flooded my mind of a very different era of my life, which was a far cry from our blessed way of living today.

I reckon I was just ten when I stood outside on a dark and bitterly cold winter evening, frozen to the core. I had very little protection against the cruel winter elements. I stood shivering in my very tatty thin dress, thin cardigan, shabby disability boots and callipers. Regardless to my immediate plight, I gazed at the beautiful blue rugged cross that seemed to be shining just for me, and it appeared to be saying, 'You're not alone.'

It was in fact the cross on the building of the Salvation Army Hall in the city, but on a dark night it looked like it was shining from the sky. It was the only few minutes of my week that I felt safe, despite what was going on in my life. There was something about my big blue cross that seemed to melt away all my troubles for just a very short time.

To be honest I am not sure if I was nine or ten. So much happened at that time in my life, so much change in just a few years that I had to learn to grow up fast. So, I knew, even at such a young age, what to do and when to do it.

I knew how to take care of lots of children, and I knew how to clean the house, or should I say, clean the pit. I knew what it was like to hear screams in the dark and I knew fear. It had become a frequent visitor to my emotions. I had to learn fast the game of survival, when to speak and when to be silent. I knew hunger, I knew fierce beatings and I knew sex. I didn't know the name of half of this stuff that was going on in my life; I just knew what to do and how to do it in my fight to survive. Looking back on it all now, it brought many unanswered questions to mind.

I was a physically and sexually abused child (nothing new in those days, so were many others.) I guess the authorities of the time did the best they could, but never-the-less, I often felt they sold thousands of kids short. It was the language they used in those days, all that professional jargon. I realized it was unintentional, but unfortunately, I couldn't help but feel that some of those words could have been responsible for what I saw as trivializing our ordeals.

Sadly, if you sell a victim sort, you're giving a break to the offender. Scrambling through the confusion of my thinking, not looking for someone to blame I may say, just seeking answers and putting it all into some form of context, I realized that no one was to blame. It was simply the way things were done, and the way things were in those days.

I can remember discussing this matter with my social worker friend many moons ago. He was telling me; the focus back then (if at all possible) was to keep the families together unless there was no choice. He said that as sad as it all was and although it was awful what many sexually abused children went through within the family environment, it wasn't looked at in the same way, as a child being abused by a stranger.

What a thought! Being abused in the home by an adult family member was seen as incest. Yet being abused by a stranger was seen as rape. I wondered what the difference was, and I was told. It was felt at the time, as unacceptable as these foul acts were to all children, that because the child knew her family member, it was not considered as emotionally horrific for them as the traumatisation of a young victim being subjected to this ordeal by a stranger.

Yes, that may have been a debatable point, but whatever way one chose to view this matter, to me it was as simple as this coming from my own place of pain, and how I saw my circumstances back then -it was the closest thing to child slavery and under aged children used for sex that I know. Nobody had to travel to third world countries to be faced with such horrors. No, it was happening in our own civilized Kingdom, in our own cities, in our very own houses and indeed in many of our families. This was a subject never spoken of aloud and always brushed under the carpets in families such as mine.

I shudder when I remember most of my childhood and recall that the only time in years, I found moments of feeling okay, was when I looked at my blue rugged cross that glowed from the dark sky. Many a time in my deepest desperation, when I got a moment where my parents were out or in a drunken heap, I sneaked out to look at it.

As I stood under the stars looking up at my bright blue cross which appeared to be beaming down on me in a reassuring way, tears started to flow down my cold pale cheeks. I pitifully looked to the heavens and though sobs of helplessness wondered, *why couldn't I see He who once hung there, and why was this happening to me?*

Back at the house I was so afraid and dreaded the sound of those steel caps shoes coming down the cobbled stone path towards what they said was my home. I knew that once *he* got inside that door, terror would reign and I was 'On the mat again,' as he called it. It was time to inflict his terrifying brutal nasties and I often trembled as I wondered whether tonight was the night that I was going to die.

I was out longer than usual this night. At the bottom of our street, over the road sitting on the curb in my shabby ill kept scrapes of clothing, my matted, thin, tatty hair hung over my pale worried little face as I snuggled into a torn, ripped, smelly army blanket, which surrounded my very underweight and undersized tiny body like a shawl.

It wasn't so long after World War II, and Great Britain was getting itself back together again, but never-the-less, the country still had much to do. Behind me was a massive bomb-pec from the German bombings on our city in war time, yet many kids found it a great and fascinating playground in spite of its dangers.

I guess I was daydreaming in my secret corner as I bravely stole a little space on this given evening. My big blue cross looked so warm and comforting from this place. Regardless to what street I stood in, my loyal friend always seemed to shine down from the sky into my face. It was as though it was trying to speak to me, to comfort me and give me a little respite from my desperate circumstances.

This particular night however, I was in deep thought, trying to fathom out in my childish mind, why was I living like this. *Why must a person have to be so hungry and afraid? Why did things have to change so much for me in my life?*

My mind drifted back to a much more joyous time of life for me. I took myself there when escaping from the reality of how bad it really was - to the memory of a time I yearned to get back to from the past. In those days I believed that by escaping into my own private fantasyland, no one could enter unless I allowed them - this act, helped to save my sanity.

It seemed that unless I was wanted to do something, go somewhere, care for kids or skivvy after someone, I don't think anyone gave a damn where I was, or what I was up to, or indeed, what was happening to me.

As long as I did not break the law of the house, which was to open my mouth and tell the truth of the horrific suffering going on behind closed doors in secret and in silence, then I was left alone. I got back a little late this particular night and to my dread *he* must have run out of beer money and was home before me.

'Hmm, where you been Peg-leg?' he sneered in that creepy vile voice which always meant I was in for it. That was me, good old reliable Peg-leg. If he was on a good day (which truly wasn't often) I was called Scabby.

'I said where have you f*****g been you little shabby Bastard?' came that voice that sent shivers down my spine as he started to remove his hob nail boot. He usually wore shoes, but he had the hob nail boots on this night. He only wore them when he earned a little 'cash in hand' working on the building sites on the quiet. Work was a disgusting word in our house, so in view of that and the never-ending drinking, it was also a rarity. Very little of his cash in hand money ever flowed into the house; it was usually spent in the pub on the way home.

So here I was again, standing across the room, frozen with fear, as this huge brute full of guilt, through his own doing, (which was drinking the money that could have fed his wife and ten children,) was as usual, focusing his shame and anger towards me.

Here we go again, Mr Nasty looking for his prey to vent his shameful, self-hatred feelings out on. Looks like Mum was getting a break tonight, and it was my turn again. That's right, somebody always copped it when he felt bad, somebody always had to pay the price for how he felt and that was almost always my mother or me.

BANG!!! The next thing I remember was my mother running along the cobbled streets with me in her arms. I could feel a tremendous pain in my head and face which seemed to be wet and sticky. Slowly coming to, returning from being knocked out by my father's hob-nailed boot, I opened my eyes and heard a desperate voice whispering quite anxiously in an almost out of breath voice, as she hurried through the dark damp night towards the hospital, 'Sally, you mustn't say your father did this, do you hear me? Don't tell them your dad did it. Promise me you won't?'

I remember looking at the wet cobbled stones glistening on the ground as the light of the dimmish streetlamp hit them. I looked up and saw in the clear dark sky, my friend, my old rugged blue cross. It seemed to shine on my face as though to hug me.

When will this ever stop? I thought.

My thoughts we're interrupted by my mother's very Irish deep breathing voice again saying urgently, 'Sally, say nothing, nothing to them about your father. Do you hear?'

'Yes Mum,' I replied in a very weak and sleepy voice. 'We'll say your brothers and sisters all attacked you okay, like a big gang fight, do you hear?'

'Yes Mum,' I responded somewhat fearful to disagree, and of course, not knowing what I know now. If only I had spoken out, it may have actually gotten me out of it all. Then again, in those days, I was soon to learn, it also may not have.

Lying on the hospital table, I remember the doctor asking how my face got into this mess. It seems my eyebrow was burst open and needed stitches. I had two huge black eyes, and the top of my lip was burst open too. In fact, that was putting it mildly, my lip was almost split in half on the right side, and my face looked like a battered, discoloured and ripped up pumpkin.

It seems I had been hit forcefully with the hobnail boot he'd slung across the room straight into my face, and immediately I'd fallen to the ground. He had knocked me clean out and when I didn't arise to his demanding command, I was fiercely attacked again while out cold on the floor. I was told later, he thought I was (in his words) 'putting it on.' My gosh, what an outrageous bully he was! What kind of state of mind was he in? To even think a child could 'put this on' while undertaking such a fierce beating was more than I could comprehend.

I heard later that my little brothers and sisters were sobbing and pleading with him to stop. A couple of the little lads threw themselves across my body and pleadingly begged him, 'Don't hurt Sally no more!' He looked at the boys as though coming to a sudden realization of his deed and stopped and ordered my mother to get me to a hospital. It was as fast and as simple as that. The outrage was over - for this night anyway.

It was me he couldn't take to; me he couldn't stand. He was great with the other kids; in fact, he adored them. He called them, 'his kids.' I was really his kid too, as it goes, I was his first born, but he couldn't bring himself to bond with me and disliked me immensely.

Why did he hate me so much? I often wondered. *Why couldn't he love me and treat me like the others? What was it about me that seemed to bring so much out of him?*

It seemed that my very presence irritated him to death. I guess many might say that there is always the one child in the family that regardless to how good they are, or how hard they try, they can never do anything right in the eyes of some. There was no doubt at all to the many who knew us, that I was the black sheep of this family.

I was very dozy as the doctor bent over my tiny, battered body and examined my swollen, bleeding wounds on my face. He continued to question my mother as though disbelieving most of what she was saying, 'Sally will have to stay in with us overnight at least. We are going to have to take an x-ray and examine the damage. I think we shall take Sally to theatre and put her to sleep while we sort out her face.'

'No doctor, her father will not like it if she stays in, I must take her home,' replied my worried about her-self Mother, who was terrified of what she might get if she returned without me.

Even so young I could understand that, but I was so relieved when the Doctor insisted to have his way. I can remember lying on the table as the nurses smiled down at me through their masks and gently said, 'You will feel a little sharp sting in a sec Sally and then you won't feel a thing I promise. Can you be a brave girl for me?'

Weakly, I smiled at her whispering yes, but deep-down thinking as I drifted off to sleep, *Brave girl - if only she knew.*

CHAPTER 2

The year 1953 was the starting of my family. Born to a young runaway in Birmingham England, was her first child Sarah, which is me. Although I was a healthy bouncing baby, my feet were deformed and this led me to spend the first seven years of my life in a Catholic orthopaedic hospital, run by nuns.

My mother was a young illiterate Irish girl who fled Ireland and her poverty-stricken parents at the age of sixteen. She had been born in the ghettos of Dublin just before the Second World War and was raised with a family of ten children.

My Grandfather, her father worked on the docks, but spent most of his life in and out of hospital suffering with chronic asthma and TB, which as time went by, eventually killed him. I was told that my mother was the apple of my grandfather's eye; he doted on her and her on him. So, as you may imagine it broke his heart when he woke one day to find her missing. They said he was never the same after that.

Grandmother was a whole different kettle of fish. No one ever said it out loud, but she was a drunk. If she wasn't drinking, she was out seeking it. When at home with her family, consisting of a sick, hardworking husband and ten boisterous kids, she was usually giving grand pops a fierce ear bashing or cocooned in a drunken heap.

My Mother being the only girl at the time, and the second eldest, was left to do most, if not all of the housework and childcare. I recall her saying how much she hated endlessly scrubbing the wooden floorboards on her hands and knees each day. But this was expected of children from families such as this in those days and she later adopted the same philosophy - when a child could walk and understand, they were ready for housework and responsibility.

Looking at an old photograph, my mother was a very beautiful young woman. She was stunningly attractive, but as time went by, I came to realize she also had an extremely low self-esteem, little self-worth, and was excessively insecure, not to say for her years, very emotionally immature.

I can imagine her stepping off the boat in Liverpool, taking a deep breath and with very little cash in her purse deciding to board the train for Birmingham. In spite of all the odds being set against her, she managed to get herself lodgings and secured herself a job in a coffee bar close by. Mother had her share of admirers too but kept herself pretty much to herself.

It was at work one Summer's evening that she first set eyes upon my father. She often spoke of that fateful night to me when I was young - the night she met the love of her life. The café was crowded as the local clan of young men and women from the neighbourhood cheerfully gathered around the pinball machine watching the players, as others shuffled about to the rocky sounds of the times from the juke box. Suddenly she noticed someone she had never seen before, but he was obviously known to the bouncy, fun-loving crowd there. Sitting by the door sat a very handsome young man who appeared to draw the interest of many a young lady there. Too little avail though.

Looking up over his coffee cup he locked eyes with my mother. He slowly lowered his cup and gave her an inviting smile, which turned her stomach upside down, sent her pulse racing and heart beating, pounding ten to the dozen. She slowly lowered her massive, beautiful eyes in shyness. It was blatant to him that this was an innocent girl.

She couldn't take her eyes off him, nor he her it seemed. So, she ke

pt herself busy about the place, in the hope that he wouldn't notice that she was attracted to him. This feeling was new and quite crazy to her, almost as if she had suddenly been bewitched. It seems he was gorgeous and charismatic (not that I saw any of that in him.)

'He could charm the knickers off a Nun,' Mum would laugh when telling the story.

'I notice the boxer has his eye on you Maria,' said one of the waitresses with a knowing wink.

'Who is he?' asked Mum blushing.

'Oh, one of the local lads. Cute hey?' she said, giving Mum a knowing look.

She saw a strength in him she admired; pride intermingled with sweetness and like a magnet she was dawn to him. So, you can imagine how she almost died on the spot when he got up from the table and walked towards the counter.

My Mother had an extremely noticeable stutter which really bothered her right now. *Oh, what would she do if he spoke to her? He would be put off,* she cringed and almost broke into a cold sweat when her panic-stricken thoughts were interrupted by a gentle cheeky voice saying, 'Hello Gorgeous, can I have another coffee?'

'Sure,' she managed to say without stuttering.

'You're not very chatty.'

She turned and smiled at him then handed him his drink.

'Do you fancy going out somewhere later?'

This was murder. *What was she going to do?* If she answered he would hear her voice, then surely, he wouldn't like her. So, she lowered her eyes sweetly and shook her head which said no.

A few days later he asked again. Then again and again but to no avail. A friend joked with her that she was playing hard to get, but this was far from the truth. She really liked him and loved his attention which flattered the socks of her. She was terrified of him hearing her stutter.

'Maria, I am going to keep asking you out until you say yes,' he told her one day while flirting with her at the café counter.

As this happened the local bully boy came in. Many sat down and were truly quite intimidated by his presence, but not my father. He continued to sweet talk Mum, who by now was withdrawing from him as she tried to discreetly disappear into the background of the café, in the hope the bully wouldn't talk to her. Her experience with him was not favourable, as he always ended up trying to make a laughingstock of her, leaving her feeling horribly humiliated.

Father, noticing she had pulled back with a worried look on her face, turned to see what the problem was. There he was the 'bully boy' walking towards the counter saying in a jeering cocky voice, 'Hey you little Irish Beauty, get that cute little ass over here and get me a coffee!'

She was nervous and got a little clumsy spilling his coffee as she rushed to serve him in her haste. She wasn't sure if it was what she knew to expect from this awful man, or the fact that she didn't want my father to hear it. To her this was a huge embarrassment.

"You stupid clumsy Moron, what's wrong with you stutters?'

He had a way with words this idiot, a right charmer, a legend in his own mind. However, he didn't impress or amuse my father at all, so spying his chance to play the knight in shining armour he said, 'That's no way to speak to a lady,' before knocking him spark out. Not to say, he was never rude to my Mum again and she went out with my dad.

My Father was also from Ireland. He and his siblings were brought to live in England by his parents when he was nine. Somehow, they had managed to get a decent comfortable home in a respectable part of Birmingham. Dad was the youngest of seven children, most of his family much older than he so they worked to support the household. He was enrolled into a respectable school nearby.

Father was the new boy on the block, not to say Irish and a target for the school bullies. Many a time he returned from school with a busted lip or black eye. This began to seriously upset my uncle, his older brother, who was an amazing tap dancer in his day. On many an occasion he often did a little shuffle to cheer dad up and tap danced for him as he sat on the back doorstep feeling sorry for himself and nursing his wounds.

One day however, Uncle decided enough was enough and grabbing my dad, he waltzed him off to a junior boys boxing club close by. By the time it was my father's tenth birthday, he had turned from the underdog at school to the cock of his year. Needless to say, school life became comfortable from then on. I often wondered in my uncle's eagerness to protect him, did he actually destroy him and do more harm?

Upon leaving school my father joined the army and after being trained, his first job was to drive the German POW to work then back to their camp. He also boxed alongside fighters such as Henry Cooper who also fought for the army. Dad was in the paratroopers and was eventually stationed in Germany for a while. Rumour has it, he fell deeply in love with young women he affectionately called his 'Frauline'.

It was Germany and the forties just after the second world war, when the British soldiers were still stationed there. My father decided he was deeply in love with this lady and told his mates he wasn't returning with them. That's right, he was thinking of absconding form the army to marry his German lover he felt he couldn't live without. Obviously, his friends tried to talk him out of it and appearing to agree with his decision they all decided to meet up for a goodbye drink a few hours before the military ship sailed back to British shores.

What my dad didn't realize though was that his friends had other plans for his life, and they got him drunk as a skunk. At the end of the night, they carried him back to the ship and before he could say a word to change it, he woke far out to sea and could do nothing about it all.

By the time he met my mother it was the beginning of the fifties. He was a builder's labourer by day and a professional boxer by night and weekends. I heard he had to box three fights a night occasionally. This would never be allowed today. It seems that if they were lucky, they could earn £25 a fight back then, which would have been a lot of money in those days.

I was also told many years ago by a boxing coach who was his friend in the boxing world back in the late forties and early fifties, that my dad used to have to travel to Leamington a few nights a week because he was chief sparring partner to Randolph Turpin on his comeback fight with Sugar Ray Robinson. Now if that was true, wow, and there was a real possibility it could have been, but I was never sure if it was nothing more than the usual chatter and Irish bullshit I was often subjected to.

I was born in May 1953, and the Queen's coronation was the excitement all over England. There were street parties and great merriment, and I received a silver spoon for being one of the babies born at such an eventful time in history.

I don't know when things started to go wrong between my mother and Father. Both wanted so much for each other. Was it when he put the ring on her finger? Was it when I was born that it all turned bittersweet? I haven't a clue. I do know though that when I was ten weeks old, it was decided by my surgeon at the Birmingham children's out-patient's department that I had to be admitted to hospital for a long and intensive period, so they could start to work on my deformities. I was sent to the infant ward of St Gerald's hospital, and this is where I recall my first memory as a child and the happiest years of my childhood.

CHAPTER 3

I knew very little of my family history whilst in hospital and I was far too young to understand anyway. I can hardly remember seeing my mother. In the seven or eight years I was there, she could have only visited three or four times in all those years. Once more, when it came to my dad, I never once met him in my early years. The fact was that I didn't even know my father existed.

The first memory I have of my mother embarrassed me. Even so young I felt embarrassed by her presence and uncomfortable in her company. I never really thought of words like Mum and Dad. Oh yes, I often heard them when other patients chatted but because I very rarely got visits myself, the words didn't really sink in. Such words meant nothing to me.

Sister Brendon the Senior Nun of our ward was the closest person to a Mother I knew back then, that was until I met my Aunty Gwen of course. Then I found out what a real Mother should be. However, that's another story I shall tell you all about later.

I look back on those early years with such fondness for they were, indeed, the happiest years of my childhood. St Gerald's was a fantastic place. The orderly, clinical, clean structure of this beautiful hospital was all I needed and loved. It was my life; the staff were my family, and this was my home.

It was a huge place with many buildings stretching across acres of land. The hospital stood in a rural area surrounded by beautiful countryside. St Gerald's hospital was set at one end of the land and Father Hudson Homes for children in care was at the opposite end. The massive building in the middle of it all was the convent. Oh, how I adored the smell of polish and that amazing feeling of peace one got on entering. It gave a wonderful feeling of security to all who entered, even to visit.

If you walked straight ahead and turned right, you'd pass all sorts of huts, there was even a tuck shop, and each hut or building had a use. Walking further forward through the grounds one came to a few rows of houses - quite a few actually. They looked like rows of bungalows but in fact they were rows of single flats, and these were the nurse's quarters.

If you were to carry on walking, bearing left you would arrive at the gigantic Catholic Church, where all the nuns, nurses, patients in wheelchairs, and children from the homes attended each Sunday and on special occasions. It was a delightful place even it if was a little daunting and creepy at times. As one continued to bear left you came upon the many houses caring for about fifteen to twenty children of all different ages run by a couple of nuns. This was Father Hudson's Homes for children in care. Facing this was the park, football pitch and about a mile of green for the use of the Homes and the able children carried by visitors from the hospital.

Across from there it looked like lower ground which went right from Father Hudson's homes all the way past the hospital wards to the other end of the grounds. One went down many stone steps to get to it. It was the farm belonging to the establishment. We were forbidden to go down there, but that never stopped us. The kids from the homes got a severe punishment when they got caught disobeying the rules. Often a good chaining and much more. I don't know anyone in the hospital but me who sneaked off down there at times, and I was hardly captured, and if so, then it was a telling off because I was in hospital. Once a person walked to the other end of the farm and back up the stone steps, they were back at the start of the grounds which was the hospital.

From this part of the land our eyes were greeted by the hospital chapel which was attached to the main hospital building. Now in this building was the baby ward and this is where I spent my baby years. Across from that was another big ward for toddlers. About four or five wards stood at this side of this part of the building and down a very long and wide corridor was a door to the left and to the right. One door led out onto the massive driveway, which took us throughout the whole of the grounds of this hospital and to the satellite wards branching off from it. The other door was really like a back door which was a playground for the little patients.

If you carried on down the corridor you would arrive at the theatres where all the surgery for every ward was done, even if the wards were not in the same building. Continuing from there was the surgery wards. We all spent time in there to be prepared for our operations and were sent back to there to recover before we returned to our main living wards. There were bathrooms, toilets, kitchens, dining rooms and a couple of classrooms for those who could get out of bed (teachers taught on the ward those who couldn't be moved.) There were also playrooms with nannies and every sort of toy you could think of. A child like I could get lost in there for ever.

Then you would arrive at the severely handicapped wards, where children with thalidomide, water on the brain, brittle bones, paraplegics, and all sorts of serious illnesses were housed. These were children that would spend their short lives in hospital, yet in spite of all that, it was a very happy and busy place.

Everywhere you looked there was a massive crucifix on the walls - in the halls, wards, in-fact every room. I knew from a very early age about Jesus dying for my sins, so I had to be a very good girl, which I rarely was even though I was a grateful to Jesus for that. As thankful as one so young could be anyway.

Leaving this building and walking across the pathway we come to our first satellite ward and that was the boy's ward, for lads from five to eleven, and the other ward joining to it housed lads from eleven to seventeen. At the back of that building was another small wooden building, which had a little swimming pool built up from the floor instead of down in the ground. This was so paraplegic girls and boys could be placed in it in body slings. This place was full off all sorts of equipment which was used for our physiotherapy. I hated going there, it was so painful for me when they worked on my feet, so I feared the place even when they took me over there to meet the famous Mr Pastry, who foolishly stood on the edge of the pool, and threw himself in to the water to the amusement of all.

We met many celebrities at this hospital doing their bit for charity, and along with them came the cameras, TV crews and newspapers. They followed them around flashing away while the celeb signed plastered legs and arms and briefly interacted with the physically disadvantaged of our society. I saw Cliff Richard, the Kay Sisters, the Beverly Sisters, Russ Conway, Helen Shapiro, and many more who aren't coming to mind right now.

At the other side of the boy's wards was a big path of green grass which had a round pond in the middle of it full of water lilies, and a splendid hanging willow tree which I loved. Across from this and completely opposite the boy's ward which was now over in the distance was seven and eight. Ward eight again was for girls aged twelve to seventeen and ward seven for girls five to eleven. The latter became my ward.

To me, the ward was my house, and the staff were my family. I saw the grounds as my garden, the patients as my friends and all of this as my home. After all, I really knew nothing else. I thrived in my little world, and in-spite of the fact that I was alone, I guess I got lots of attention from staff and visitors. The little girl on the ward who never got a visitor, in my case was not a little girl forgotten. I was a happy child who knew love and security and I bloomed in my environment.

Thinking back though I clearly recall something that was a little different about me. I liked the company of women but was never at ease with the attention or company of men. I was fine with my surgeon Mr Allen who I had known since a baby and of course, the Priest. After those two, I had a strange attitude and discomfort with and towards men.

I recall a time back then when a young married couple started to visit me. They didn't come for long and after a time they were allowed to take me out for the day. I don't recall when I met them or how. Most likely they would have been visiting someone else. If there were more than three visitors to a bed, the staff nurse removed them, and they were often enticed to visit the little girl who never got visitors – me.

Well, when the young lady didn't visit me, her husband did. I remember him coming one Saturday afternoon in visiting hours - 2pm to 4 pm and this particular day he took me out for walk. I couldn't walk so he carried me. He took me into the nearby village and to the church there. He carried me up the long and winding stone steps to the steeple so we could look out at the beautiful surrounding countryside.

Do you know it's strange really, how someone can remember a thought or identify a feeling from days of old, but they cannot recall any incident to make them feel that way. This is the first time I recall one of the most uncomfortable and frightening feelings that I had as a child and I don't know what triggered it. I remember this young man carrying me up to the steeple and for some reason I felt very uncomfortable and panicky and sobbingly asked him to take me back. I just wanted to get away from him. I remember him trying to cheer me up and buying me an ice cream on the way back. I do not remember anything at all nasty happening with the young man, but I never ever saw him again. I think I was about five at the time.

Do you know I had never used the words 'Mummy' or 'Daddy' back then? I am not sure if I even knew what a Mummy and Daddy truly meant - mainly because I had no recollection of ever meeting them. Yes, I knew of these words that seemed to come so naturally to the other children, and I knew they called the people who usually visited them. For me though, I simply thought a Mummy and Daddy was someone or something I hadn't got. It would seem that because I had grown to this age without them, I didn't miss them or expect them, however I yearned at times for a visitor of my own. As naturally as 'Mummy and Daddy' came to the children, the words 'Sisters Brendon, nurse and doctor' seemed to come naturally to me.

When I was in the ward for patients up to the age of five in the main hospital building, the young Nun in charge of that ward was Sister Pauline. I believe she had nursed me and mothered me since a baby, and I was so attached to her. She would carry me everywhere with her even into the convent. One day she took me over to another ward, ward seven for five- to eleven-year-old girls. I remember meeting what I thought was an old nun. They took me into the office and as I sat on my Sister Pauline's lap I was gently introduced to Sister Brendon and told I would be moving into her ward and her care now. This meant I wasn't going to have Sister Pauline.

I went berserk and clinging to her begged her not to leave me. It was as hard for Sister Pauline as it was for me. She promised to visit me and for a few weeks she did every day. After a few weeks it got less and less until finally it was once a month. The last time I saw her she sat me one her knee to tell me she had to move to another convent a very long way away and couldn't come anymore. I was so upset, but as you do, I eventually got over it and Sister Brendon began to take the major womanly role in my life.

CHAPTER 4

Ward Seven brings back many pleasant memories. This place was my palace and I adored it. One of my favourite places to lose myself in was its gardens. The nurses always knew where to find me if I wasn't in my bed on a warm day. Normally I got out of bed, and hopped on one leg, or crawled on my bum to get to where I wanted to be. Often it was to make my way to the front of the ward and out into the ward garden.

This was a special time for me in the Summer. I could always be found crawling around the gardens or sitting with my garden ornaments which were alive, my friends and very real to me. I guess today they would have been called my imaginary friends. I enjoyed the pleasantry of it all for many hours as I quietly played away, admiring the vibrant colours, and soaking in the full beauty of what I saw as my little paradise - the most beautiful place in the world to me.

I would crawl around it looking at the different range of flowers growing up the sloped flowerbed to the hedge and gaze continuously at the many different coloured flowers that took my fancy. That was of course until I decided to chat to my friend Mr Gnome, a lovely little fellow to my childish mind - jolly with brightly coloured clothes and big smiling face and lovely red hat

Another place I would hop off to was the ward next door, ward eight which housed twelve- to eighteen-year-olds. I spent a great deal of time on this ward - I was quite forward for my years so a lot of the time looked forward to my time with the older girls even though most of the time I ended up driving them cuckoo. I guess it was Rose who took me under her wing a bit.

She would have been a tall girl if she could have stood up and wasn't held back by her wheelchair and callipers which actually went from the top of her legs to her handicapped brown strapped boots. She couldn't walk alone and never without callipers, and it seemed never would. Rose had polio.

I thought the world of Rose and she seemed to look upon me as a little sister. As soon as I approached her bed, she would bid me to get on and help me up - it was always a struggle for us both. Even though she had weak and worthless legs her arms were very strong. We would often end up full of giggles as we took on this get me on the bed task. Rose spent a great deal of time Mothering me which she fully enjoyed and took that task with full responsibility. I guess for what little I knew about love, I loved her. I loved my daily visits to that ward - as well as chatting to my many friends and receiving from them the attention I demanded at times. I also hopped around doing errands for many of them and my biggest task was nipping down to the farm to deliver a love letter to the farmer's boy whom my friend Mary was in love with.

Not receiving visitors of my own, I felt very lonely during visiting hours. I would make the usual round of my friend's parents and receive my sweets and the attention I often yearned. I was a nice child, mischievous but a little girl many would have wanted. I guess I was a proper little madam that people seemed to like having around - either that or they greatly pitied me. I tried to be pleasant and was nearly always sweetly cheeky but very cheerful. But at times, I could not help envying my friends for being so lucky and having the same people to visit them each week.

At this stage of my life my greatest wish was to have someone of my own to visit me and love me as those other children. Not that the nurses didn't make a fuss of me - some of them came over at visiting hours at their time off with their boyfriends who along with them would take me out.

I remember one of the boyfriends visited me for a long while, almost every week; most times he came alone, he would buy me sweets and carry me down the village to see the shops, then off to the park for a little while, then he would take me to the top of the church steeple. I loved that, and liked him very much, but could not help feeling uneasy with him when alone. I cannot remember how long he came for, but I do know suddenly his visits stopped. Then a policeman and his wife started to visit me, and my previous friends slowly drifted into the background. I suppose I was spoiled really.

By now I'd had four or five operations. I had club feet you see. The last operation I had was behind my knee, which seemed strange seeing that it was supposed to be my feet that had the problem, not my legs as well. I am sure that there was more wrong here than I ever knew about. On one occasion when I had yet another operation on my foot, I was plastered from my toes to my knee.

For me, this was great, I could hop around as much as I wanted and even the extra weight of the plastered leg, never bothered me at all. I hated being bed ridden, because I was so full of life and as I said I had a cheeky mischievous personality. The nurses called me 'A right little rogue,' while Sister Brendon called me her 'little Scallywag.' In-spite of my circumstances I was a contented, happy, and thriving little girl.

Our Christmas' in hospital were fantastic. Everything was laid on for us. The trimmings were massive and plentiful in our huge ward. A stage would be built at one end of the ward, with big cardboard Disneyland figures, and at the side of it was a big Christmas tree full of everything a child could imagine. I can still remember how it sparkled beautifully of an evening when its lights were on. We were taken to pantomimes but mostly they came to us for wonderful ward parties full of music, food, chatter, and children shouting in excitement as they ate and opened their gifts. Radio broadcasters came in and had live shows on the wards. They'd go around talking to the kids, getting them to say a poem, play the flute, maybe sing a little song; whatever they could do really. The newspapers came around at party time and took photographs of us with Father Christmas. Groups of people from various charities came along bringing lots of presents. There was never a dull moment as something was always going on throughout Christmas.

My little world was built around this hospital; even though it was a long-stay orthopaedic hospital, with unpleasant sights, we were happy and adored it. The policeman and his wife came to see me regularly by now. They started to take me home for days and then I started to stay for weekends. I remembered feeling so proud of my Uncle Bob (as I called him) because he was a policeman. I used to ask him to come and see me in his uniform, which he did. We built up a great relationship and I was very fond of them.

Days, weeks, and months rolled by and there was still no sign of my mother, but I did not mind. I only remembered seeing her once before and I did not know who she was then.

One weekend I went home with the policeman and his wife. When we returned on the Sunday, Sister Brendon told us I could not go again for a while because my mother had been to see me while I was out and had kicked up a huge fuss. She'd left orders that I was not allowed out with other people again. Mr and Mrs Ball still came to see me though. I resented not being allowed out for weekends, and I guess it began to show itself in my behaviours. I got a little nasty and spiteful to the other kids in my ward when they upset me.

Sister Brendon was someone special in my life. Apart from treatment, she spent more time with me than the other children. She would come over in her spare time and take me for walks. She always had sweets in her pocket for me and chatted to me about almost anything trying to answer the inquisitive questions a six or seven-year-old would ask.

I remember asking her one day, 'Sister, are you my Mummy?'

'No, Sarah.'

'Why?' I asked.

'God gave you your own Mummy Sarah.'

'Who is that then Sister?

'The lady with all those children who came to see you that time.'

'If she is my Mummy, why doesn't she come a lot like all the other Mummies?'

'I've told you Sarah, she lives a very long way away from here, and she has all your little family to look after,' Sister Brendon replied.

'Yes, I know that Sister, but I don't like her. I don't want her for my Mummy, I want you!'

Sister Brendon went very quiet at this and passed it off knowing that no matter what she said, there was no way that I would accept the woman she spoke of as my mother. I asked her some tricky questions at times, but she always had an answer for me and left me feeling contented. I asked her one day, 'Sister how did I get here?' To which she replied, 'Jesus sent you Sarah!' All day I tried to remember Jesus sending me here and I couldn't so I went back to Sister Brendon saying, 'I have been thinking all day and I can't remember Jesus sending me Sister?'

Now she knew better than to keep feeding me this one for I would never let it go. So, she replied, 'Sarah, Jesus did send you but you actually came from your Mummy's tummy - you know the lady with all the other little children?' I frowned in confusion at all of this. 'Why did Jesus put me in her tummy Sister? I don't like her.'

'Because he did Sarah, she is your Mummy.'

'But I don't know her Sister, I don't like them!'

'Well Sarah, she is your Mummy, and they are your brothers and sisters, and you will have to get used to that dear,' she said, waltzing off and patting me on the head as she did so. For days I thought about this one and on catching Sister Brendon walking by one day, I grabbed her hand asking as we walked together (me hopping of-course), 'Sister, I can't remember Jesus putting me in the lady's tummy? How did I get there?'

Hmm this one took her by surprise and with this answer she was trying to kill many birds with one stone. She sat down put me on her knee and softly said, 'Sarah my dear, you are a beautiful little girl, a true gift from God so Jesus gave you to your Mummy and Daddy.'

'What's a Daddy Sister?'

'You know Sarah, the men that come with the Mummies to visit your friends in the ward.'

'But I've never seen one come to me Sister, not even with that strange lady with those smelly scruffy children that come before.'

'That's right dear you haven't so how about if we go to the tuck shop and get you some lovely ice cream?'
'Yes, thank you Sister Brendon,' I said excitedly, forgetting all about my questions for now, as she put me in the wheelchair and pushed me off to get my ice cream.

CHAPTER 5

I woke one day to the sound of children singing Happy Birthday to me. On my locker stood cards and gifts, and after they had finished singing Sister Brendon came to my bed, 'Good morning scallywag and happy birthday to you!' she said. 'Come on, wake up dear, it's your birthday! You're six years old today!'

'Am I Sister?' I said shaking the sleep from my eyes. 'I'm really six! Gosh! I'm getting a big girl now, aren't I?'

'You most certainly are!' she laughed. 'Now come on let's see what your presents are,' she said, sitting on the bed and beginning to help me open them.

'Sister Brendon - what does it mean being six years old today?' I asked curiously. I couldn't understand why I was being made such a fuss of today.

She thought for a moment as if I had taken her quite by surprise, then after a moment she said gently, 'Sarah, dear - this day six years ago your mother gave birth to you.'
'What does that mean, Sister?' I asked quite bewildered with it all.

'It means that the lady who comes to see you at times, brought you into the world and that's how you came to be here,' she explained.

'Where did she get me from then?' I persisted.

'From her tummy dear, you are the blessing from God.'

'But how did Father God get me in her tummy? Has God put a baby in my tummy?'

Clearing her throat and starting to look uncomfortable she said, 'Well - you are a little inquisitive one, Sarah! God gave you to her like he gives all little children - in a way - to their Mummies and that's why you all have your own Mummies because God gives you to one special Mummy that is just right just for each little child.'

'Like Our Lady, Sister?' I said, meaning Mary, the mother of Jesus. I was always fascinated with pictures of Mother Mary holding her baby Jesus. I saw many on the walls throughout the hospital.
'In a funny sort of way Sarah,' she replied.

'Then I came from her tummy?' I asked and went on to add, 'I've seen the picture Bible book and Father God sent the angel to put the baby Jesus into Our Ladies tummy by magic – right Sister?'

'How clever you are dear - heaven knows what you will tell me on your seventh birthday!' Sister Brendon laughed, quite amused as she toddled off to prepare my special day. I may not have had the same as the other kids in the hospital at times, but Sister Brendon did a great job of going to any lengths in making sure I never went without or got forgotten.

I was one of those children - the more I was told, the more doors opened in my mind and the more I wanted to know. I received a great deal of attention from both staff and patients and even so young they encouraged my curiosity which turned me into a very intelligent and forward child. Sister Brendon felt that I would be very clever one day if pushed in my schooling. We had school in the ward and homework, plus the older patients and sometimes the staff encouraged me in schoolwork and often helped me.

I was also a gamey little dancer on my one leg. I loved music and I loved dancing. Sister Brendon was quite proud of it to and would often bring the groups of charity visitors to see me dance the twist to Chubby Checker.

Come Christmas, Easter and my birthday, those people would ask us what we might like for our Birthdays and Christmas. They would send all the children gifts and to our amazement everything we had requested. Come to think of it, we had very expensive taste and always received the latest fad in toys.

I continued to ask Sister Brendon questions about myself and estranged family. Soon, the questions that I endlessly asked her became even more than she could answer, and she would caringly divert the conversation away from my mother. The truth was, she never had the answers. I recall saying to her this day of my Birthday, 'I don't really understand what you are saying to me Sister - and I don't like you to keep telling me that poor lady who I can't really remember much is my Mummy. She's poor and scruffy and Jesus wouldn't put me in a poor lady's tummy. Mummies look after a child, but she never looks after me. Does Jesus give you to Mummies to look after you then?'

'No Sarah just one but sometimes some Mummies are very busy and someone else may have to look after their children for a while. I guess some children think of these other people taking care of them as Mummies at times,' came the answer.

'Then you're my Mummy, I must have come from your tummy Sister?' I reasoned.

'No, Sarah dear, Nuns do not have children,' she said with a very loving expression on her face. 'I look after you because you have poorly feet and legs, so for a while you must stay in hospital - but you belong to your mother dear. Please try to believe that. You must learn that one day you will go home to your own home to live with your Mummy and family.'

This deeply disturbed me, 'No, I won't go there - I'll never leave you and I'll never leave here – I will cry until I make myself die if you ever let that poor lady take me home. I love you and if you let me ever be taken away it means you don't love me and you love me very much don't you Sister?' I desperately pleaded, staring up at her as I clung to her habit seeking her comfort and some reassurance. I couldn't understand how somebody I did not like or even know could come and take me away if they wanted – remove me from this place I loved so much, from this environment where I was surrounded by so much love, cleanliness, and beauty.

This was the only place I knew as home, and these were the only people I knew as family. I was adored, well cared for, wore beautiful clothing (supplied by the hospital in my case I may add.) My hair was always combed and shining with pretty, colourful ribbons.

The boots or shoes I wore were strong and always polished. I sat at the children's table for breakfast, dinner, teatime and supper and said my grace. I had perfect manners for a child my age. The only 'violence' we knew was the odd smack when a squabble spilled over, or something very naughty had happened. Yes indeed, I was an exceptionally blessed child who, regardless to the truth of my life, wanted for nothing.

This was my world - the world that I wanted and the only world that I felt safe in, a world that I understood and came to love very much. I never dreamed or even thought a day might come whereby I would leave - I just presumed that I would always stay here until I grew up like Sister Brendon, then I would get married to God like she did and become a Nun myself. The thought that someone could ever come and take me away forever deeply distressed me.

'Don't cry now Sarah, of course I love you,' Sister Brendon said. 'It's your birthday - come on let's see what presents you have, and we shall not talk about this anymore today!'

But I was distraught and wouldn't let it go, 'Promise you won't ever let anybody take me away then, Sister,' I begged, 'Please promise!' I cried clinging to her.

I couldn't understand why Sister Brendon said this to me at times, she knew it was so upsetting for me; I simply couldn't and wouldn't accept it. The thought that I had a Mummy that was going to take me away one day, frightened me to death and created great unrest in me.

'Don't worry too much about that now Sarah, nobody is going to take you away at the moment- now look at this beautiful doll somebody has brought you, isn't she lovely?'

The distraction seemed to work and as I focused on my new dolly I replied, 'Yes, she is Sister; I've never seen a doll like this before she is black like my friend Brenda. Brenda and her Mummy and Daddy brought it for me.'

Brenda was West Indian, had brittle bones and was my best friend. We had been friends for years and we both lived on ward seven. Apart from our noticeable disabilities we were pretty much like any other little girl friends. We shared things, played games because we had a lot in common and even fought together when we disagreed at times. The only trouble was if I hit her hand in our rows, better still if she hit mine, her arm would break and have to be plastered because of the brittle bones.

We got into trouble for it though so when we got angry, we tried to do one quick pull of each other's hair. However, Brenda, being wheelchair bound, couldn't always get her pull, because I was a very fast hopper and when I gave her an angry tug I hurriedly hopped off. Nevertheless, this never lasted for long, and we were great friends more often than not.

'Brenda thank you for my beautiful baby doll - she's so pretty and black just like you – I will keep her forever to always remind me of you,' I cheerfully shouted across the ward to my little friend who was smiling at the pleasure she could see her gift had given me. She seemed to like the idea that the doll looked like her and that one day she would get one that looked like her roguish full of fun friend – little me!

We opened the rest of my gifts, and I got a little more excited with each one. How I wished that it was my birthday every day. All too soon we came to the end of my gifts. I was thrilled with all my new toys and boxes of sweets I had received but my highlight of the day was the pretty dress that Sister Brendon had brought me. She had taken me out of the ward to her office to show me my dress and get me ready. She bathed me and dried my hair putting a beautiful ribbon in it to match my dress and when all dressed up and feeling a million dollars, she waltzed me off back to the ward. I was the birthday girl and I loved it.

CHAPTER 6

On opening the ward door, I hopped for joy and screeched in excitement at what greeted me. Oh, what a thrill this really was. I could not believe my eyes when I saw what was awaiting me. The ward was filled with music as a nurse acted as DJ at the record player. The children were in their beds with party hats on and trays full of lovely party food and crackers on their lockers. The bedridden were doing the hand-jive, laughing, and chatting away merrily as the other children who could get out of bed sat around the biggest party table I'd ever seen in my life. It was beautiful and very colourful - full of jellies, cakes, biscuits, sweets, crackers, flowers, and balloons - simply everything a child could want and imagine.

In the middle of the table sat the biggest birthday cake I had ever seen with six pink candles on top. I was overjoyed and could have died of excitement; I couldn't remember ever feeling so happy in my life. The party was brilliant and all in all it was surely one of the grandest parties that I'd seen there.

The two wards came together to enjoy the festivities, while parents created a long line then started dancing through both wards. It was so funny as they all danced past us in their bright coloured paper party hats. I was the belle of the ball, and I soaked in every bit of it. This was surely the finest time of my life. Everybody I adored was there - Sister Brendon, Dr Allen, the Priest, the nurses, my friends, their parents and the police man and his wife Mr and Mrs Ball.

In fact, they had brought the cake and had a great deal to do with putting my party together. I don't think a child could have felt more loved and wanted. This was a fine party with great merriment, and everyone was having a brilliant time. I gazed around almost stunned at the fine party table, which was almost as big as the ward, and even seeing all this with my own eyes I still found it hard to believe this was all for me - a real birthday party of my own.

Brenda and I sat together fooling around, giggling while she helped me open even more gifts. I had never seen so many presents for one person before and it was so wonderful. Everything was going fine as the music blared, laughter filled the room and excited children shouted with joy. Sister Brendon lit the six candles on the lovely big cake, and everyone sang happy birthday. I felt like a Princess and loved all this attention.

Then, Uncle Bob picked me up in his arms giving me a lovely Fatherly hug as everyone shouted and clapped hip-hip-hurray six times. Uncle Bob bent down for me to blow out the candles and we pulled a few crackers and got stuck into the table full of colourful goodies. Uncle Bob told somebody to play the piano, 'Come on, Sarah, sing us a song?' he asked me.

'I can't, I'm eating,' I said stuffing my face with some more cake.

'Oh, but you can dear, can't she Sister Brendon?'

'Of course, I think that would be nice,' she replied, giving me an encouraging expression.

'Oh, go on, Sarah, sing please, Sarah!' shouted the children.

'No, I can't, I feel silly,' I said having an unusual moment of embarrassment.

'Don't be daft, come on Sarah, I'll give you a shilling,' said Uncle Bob, determined to get his way; knowing I was money mad - money meant ice cream, pop, and sweets. The ward went quiet, apart from the piano, as I started to sing in my un-shy little girl way the song Sister Brendon had heard from me many times before.

'Caroline-a-moo keep shining - shining on the one who waits for me. Caroline-a-moo I'm lonely - lonely for the one who waits for me. Let's go to the bright window - go to the right window - Stand on my right - I'll stay there all night for you - you - Caroline-a-moo I'm lonely - so lonely for the one who waits for me.'

Oh my, you could hear a pin drop as many wiped away a tear, anyone could see I had truly touched many hearts at that moment, more so I guess due to the knowledge of my circumstances. Everyone started cheering and clapping. Uncle Bob hugged me, and his wife kissed me, both seemed a little choked. Sister Brendon seemed quite touched. They all clapped and cheered louder. I felt like a popstar!

Suddenly everything went silent. I looked around, bewildered by the sudden change in atmosphere. Following the adult's eyes to the end of the table I saw the reason for their silence. It was that lady again, the one from my bad dreams. The one who Sister Brendon said was my Mummy that would take me away one day. I panicked – oh what was I to do? She was surrounded by four scruffy, dirty, tatty, poverty-stricken looking children whose eyes bulged with excitement and disbelief at this fine big party they'd suddenly walked into. The woman looked much the same as I remembered. She looked unkept, as though she needed to take care of herself. She looked tired, sad, and carried wrinkles of worry across her forehead.

'Hey Nun give us some cake would ya, look there's stacks left?' asked one of the children to my great embarrassment. Everything about this family brought me great discomfort and I simply didn't want to be associated with them. The girl continued to play up and began getting loud and very disruptive which annoyed me and stressed me to a further level. Her Mother gave her a clatter across the head which only seemed to make this crude little beast even angrier.

'You wait till I got you home girl,' her mother told her before Sister Brendon came to the rescue.

'Of course you can have a cake dear,' she said. 'Nurse, get Mrs. Murphy a seat and get someone to hold the baby to give her a rest for a moment – also bring a nice cup of tea and some food for her and get more staff to take these little ones to the party table so Mum can spend a little time with Sarah.'

Her orders brought a sense of normality back to the room.

'Here, you come with me as well dears,' she said, taking one of little ones by the hand and taking them along to the table. The children piled their plates high with food whilst also stuffing their mouths and filling their pockets as they plundered away stealing my party food. Obviously, they had no manners at all - at the same time as all this shouting to each other with a mouth full of food and swearing away as they did to the shock and horror of all. I called Uncle Bob and whispered to him to look at those greedy children stealing things off my party table for I was astounded by what I was seeing, 'They are thieves, like you said once. People who steal are called thieves! Put them in jail for it, they are stealing! I'm not going to my party table while they keep stealing Uncle Bob!' I said in horror.

'They are not stealing really, Sarah dear,' he explained. 'They've never seen a party as lovely as this, so they are just excited. They don't think that they are doing any wrong. Besides they are your little sisters, Sarah dear, and have come all this way to see you. So, you don't really want them to go to jail do you?'

'Okay,' I muttered! *It's a shame really, they are so poor* I thought to myself.

'Good girl, Sarah,' he said. 'Shall we go and say hello to your Mummy again?'

A deep uneasiness came over me, 'No, I don't like her,' I replied.

'Sarah, please talk to your Mummy,' he said holding my hand. 'She's come a very long way to see you, let's go and see her!'

'Yes, but I don't want to Uncle Bob, please don't make me, please!' I replied, as the tears began to flow. Uncle Bob seemed to sense what I was feeling so changed the subject. I decided that if I ignored them, they might just go away so started to chat away with Bob and his wife. Somebody put the music back on and my friends were all enjoying the party again. One of my siblings ran over to the table and to my surprise lifted the end of her dress and filled it full of cakes, sweets, biscuits and whatever she could, before running back to my mother who put it in a white plastic bag. This seemed to amuse the staff and adults who saw it, so she did it again, only this time seemed happy with what she'd got so plonked herself down on the floor eating away merrily. The other little ones walked around the table also stuffing things in their mouths and pockets.

I couldn't begin to understand all this for I had been taught that this was stealing and very bad manners. Their behaviour and manners appalled me. Yet it didn't seem to upset Sister Brendon or my guests at all, so I decided to take no notice and try to enjoy myself, hoping that they would all go away shortly.

No such luck. I watched out of the corner of my eye as Mother got up and came down the side of the table towards me. I stopped what I was doing and grabbed Uncle Bob's arm in fear. She held her arms out, hoping I would go to her, which of course she had no chance of happening.

Sister Brendon, sensing that this situation might soon get out of hand, came over and started to talk to me, gently trying to coax me to go to my Mummy, at the same time throwing a smile towards my mother in the hope to keep her calm and this problem under control. I didn't want to know and wasn't going to have any of it. For Sister Brendon's sake eventually, I mumbled hello.

'Sally, I'm your Mummy – will you give your mammy a hug?' she said attempting to prise me off Uncle Bob's knee. I only clung on tighter, determined never to let go.

'She's not my Mummy, is she Uncle Bob?' I pleaded. 'Please don't let her take me!'

His wife came over and putting her arms around me she gently tried to coax me, 'Let your mother hold you for a minute, Sarah. She's come such a long way to see you.'

'No, no please, she frightens me,' I said beginning to panic. 'I don't want her to hold me. Tell her to go away now, please.' I began to sob, dreading them forcing me into her arms, 'My name is Sarah, not Sally,' I said as my stomach started churning. I don't know what it was but there was something about this name Sally, that I hated, and I did not want to be called it by this woman.

'Yes, that's right, but we all call you Sally at home.'

'Sarah, this lady is your mother,' Uncle Bob said gently. 'You must understand that dear.'

'No, no, send her away, please, oh please make her go now,' I said becoming hysterical.

'It's alright, Sarah, nobody is going to hurt you dear,' said Bob's wife.

'Can I have a word?' interrupted Sister Brendon, taking Mother to one side. 'I realise how this must hurt you Mrs Murphy but I'm sure that in time Sarah will get use to you. She cannot understand all this right now – maybe if you could visit more, Sarah will come to know you as her mother.'

The facts of that truth seem to really annoy her and with a sudden burst of anger as if searching for the words to also hide her embarrassment she yelled at Sister Brendon in her uneducated, common Dublin accent, 'F*** off you cheeky ole Bastard, talking to me like that - and you a Nun and all - don't you even think about accusing me of forgetting about my child!'

'That is not what I am implying Mrs Murphy. I understand your circumstances. I am simply trying to be helpful and suggest if it was possible to see you a little more it would help you and Sarah to come to know each other better.'

'It's all your fault and who are those two holding my Sally?' she said rounding on Uncle Bob and his wife. 'She's my f***ing daughter you know - so put her down now!' She was getting more and more aggressive and very loud. I had never heard such words as the F and B word before in my life. They were so strange to me I couldn't even say them. I thought they were some sort of strange new language.

Many tried to intervene and calm it all down - for by now it was beginning to cause a lot of confusion and chaos in the ward which was distressing the other patients. Mother seemed to have little regard for that though - she wasn't stopping and continued to vent her outrageous rage at all these beautiful people. In-fact it got worse, 'You lot are poisoning my child's mind against me,' she shouted almost in tears.

'Now, now that's simply not true Mrs Murphy - let's go to my office have a cup of tea and chat about all this,' Sister Brendon said.

'My kid won't come near me and it's your fault,' she said. 'Call yourselves Christian people? Nuns my arse!'

A lady visitor confronted her and asked could she stop shouting and swearing in front of her child, 'You're terrifying the children. Stop it please!'

As if it couldn't get worse Mother shouted in answer, 'Make me stop if you can, now F off and mind your own business.'

Another Mother began to get seriously peed off at my mother's attitude and selfish behaviour and seemed to have gone past the point of watching others trying to reason with her. So, she walked over to my mother and straight to her face gave her a few home truths, 'Mrs Murphy, you dare to stand here accusing everybody for everything that's gone wrong for you. You refuse to accept any of this as your fault. I have been coming here three times a week from Birmingham and that's as far as you have to travel, and by bus - for over a year to visit my little girl and I have other children too! In all that time I never seen you ever visit your child.

'Now how can you expect little Sarah to know you? Yet you come in here shouting screaming, being rude to Sister Brendon, frightening the children and spoiling your daughter's birthday party. You should be ashamed of yourself. Your behaviour is disgusting.'

Well, that was it, all hell let lose. My Mother went berserk swearing and trying to attack the lady who told her off. Other people ran into the ward to see what the commotion was all about. In her rage she tried making a grab for me. I screamed; panic stricken.

With this, the whole ward erupted. The other young patients cried for her to go away. My little siblings were screaming. I remember screaming as my mother launched herself at Uncle Bob's wife and she began to wreck what was left of my party table. It was then that Sister Brendon grabbed me and rushed me out of the ward. The last memory I have of my mother that day was her shouting like a wild woman, 'You can stick your party up your arses - my kid doesn't need your stuff! I want my kid – get her now!'

CHAPTER 7

It took me while to get over that day but eventually with no further visits I began to relax and tried to forget all about her. Uncle Bob never came to see me again after that. I could not understand that. I felt the loss of his visits and found it hard to come to terms with his sudden absence. I realize now, him being a policeman, he was most likely ordered by his superiors to let me go and back off.

As the months continued to pass by, I persisted in asking Sister Brendon about Uncle Bob. As hard as Sister Brendon gently tried to help me get over this and come to terms with it, I still refused to accept what she was saying,

'I want you to be a brave girl for me now Sarah,' she said one day when I was particularly upset.

'I know how unhappy you feel at times my little one - but always remember child, I love you and Sister Brendon is always here with you. And look at Jesus on the picture up there Sarah. Jesus loves you very much too and when you are sad, he knows that too my dear, and He also becomes very sad because the Lord hurts when you hurt. He will always be with you, every day of your life, regardless to where you are or what you do. This I promise you Sarah, He will never leave you or forsake you.'

'But I can't see Jesus Sister. I know my Jesus is there but why can't I see Him?'

'He is Spirit. Trust in Jesus, tell him when you are sad or hurt, even when you are happy, he'll always be listening even though at times it may not seem that way. Now never forget what old Sister Brendon taught you this day – for a day will come where I fear you will truly need to lean on these words.'

I hadn't got a clue what she was talking about and as time passed by, I settled into my old routine, getting used to the fact that I was the little child of the ward that didn't get visits. It became something I learned to live with quite easily. I had been in St Gerald's most of my life now and I could only think of this Nun as the most wonderful person I have ever known in my life. I loved her dearly and even now; I think of her with the greatest warmth and love.

Time flew by with still no sign of my mother - not that I wanted to see her anyway. Another couple began to visit me - Auntie Gwen and Uncle George. Aunty Gwen brought some much-needed joy into my life and became someone so special to me.

I fell in love with Auntie Gwen almost at once. She seemed so caring, kind and loving and as time went by, I doted on her, adoring the constant attention and love she brought to me. Even after only a few visits I felt I had found somebody who was going to love me for ever. It was clear I was loved and treated as one of her own. As the seasons passed by, Aunty Gwen and Uncle George came on every visit and took me home for weekends and even had me along on their holidays. I loved the seaside even though I was afraid of the sea because of all that water, yet I loved the beach and all in all, those fun days became some of my fondest and most treasured memories.

My seventh birthday came, and Aunty Gwen had a beautiful big party for me, with a lovely birthday cake all made of ice cream. All the girls on their birthdays got bought this beautiful nylon dress which was the height of fashion at the time and to my excited delight, Aunty Gwen and Uncle George had brought me one for my party too. Here I was again, the belle of the ball and I was overwhelmed with joy. Thankfully, there were no intrusions from my family this time and it turned out to be the most wonderful day.

I had undergone quite a few operations by this time and was starting to be introduced to some new callipers. What I hated at this stage was my nighttime callipers and bed boots. The boots had metal soles with rings on the toe and another loop on the strap of the calliper around my knees which when fastened would pull the strap from the toe hoop to the knee hoop straightening my feet while I slept. When the nurse put them on and pulled that strap it really hurt and ached until I fell asleep, and to think I had to wear them in bed all night.

I was seven now and starting to learn to walk. One day when the doctor was examining me, I did my usual struggle to limp a few steps; he began to frown a little and turned to Sister Brendon saying, 'The time has come for another operation so Sister would you please make contact with Sarah's parents and ask for their written consent for surgery? Do express to them the importance of this operation and that we want and need to get it done soon. Sarah is the perfect age for this now.'

'Of course, doctor, I'll do that tonight, Sister replied as they walked on to the next bed together.

I heard nothing more on this matter until a few months later. It was the early hours of the morning when the nurses did one of their 'strip changes', where they change the sheets and remake all the beds in the ward. I always went mad and cried when they woke me so one nurse always had to hold me, pacifying me while the other did the bed. This night I was awake before they got to my bed and heard them chatting away.

'Little Sarah Murphy next. Bet she'll wake the ward - a cute little thing though, isn't she? I feel so sad for her not having a family that bothers about her since the day she came into hospital as a baby.'

'I know very sad indeed,' came the reply. 'I heard she's due more surgery but when they wrote to her parents for consent it seems the letter was returned saying, "Moved - new address unknown." Can you imagine a mother moving leaving her child in hospital and not informing them of their whereabouts?'

'I know!' replied the other nurse. 'I believe Sister Brendon has written to the social services that know of the family and will be taking the papers for consent.'

This grasped my interest and I said, 'Are you talking about me Nurse?'
'Oh no Sarah dear – come on Sweetie let's get you up while we do your bed.'

I wasn't a silly child, and I knew that they were. This is the sort of thing you hear in jokes. You know much like, what's the height of rejection, sending your child to the shop for something then moving while their gone. Can you believe it? It could only happen to me. My invisible parents had left me in hospital and moved without informing the ward of their new address. If it wasn't so sad it would have been ridiculously funny. Personally, I didn't care at all if I never saw them again. In fact, this suited me nicely. For now, I had started to learn that the unkempt looking lady with those scruffy rude children really was my Mummy but regarding a Daddy, I didn't think I had one.

Life went on; I had my surgery and seeing that I was very much on the mend unfortunately it was back to the bed callipers for a while, but the good news was that I was fitted for my own daily callipers and special boots. I was going to walk and have my own new boots and callipers. Oh, this was so exciting. It took about a month with them drawing and measuring my feet, but all too soon, to my delight my new boots arrived. I was determined not to walk in my new boots and callipers until Aunty Gwen and Uncle George arrived to visit me in a few days, and I didn't, plus to my joy, none of the staff made me. They happily agreed to allow me to do this.

That Saturday afternoon I got the nurse to put my new boots and callipers on and then cover me up with a small blanket to hide it so I could surprise my visitors. Aunty Gwen and Uncle George arrived to visit me as usual. As they came to my bed, after hugging them I made them cover their eyes and sang 'da-da-da-da' as I ripped my cover off, 'Surprise!' I screeched with excitement as they hugged and kissed me sharing my joy. For the rest of the afternoon, with me in the centre of them, they each had an arm and walked me around the long ward.

A few times I was asked to take a little rest, but no, not me, this was a new thing I was doing – walking - and nothing and no-one was going to stop me. What more could a little girl want? I had it all in this environment which had come to mean so much to me - inspite of the few events of old which had brought me great stress and the fact that I had really gone through quite a lot physically for such a little person. I was almost eight years old now with the mind of a forty-year-old one might say jokingly.

Just eight yet I could carry a conversation with anyone and keep my ground when stating my point. I could chat as a child with children my own age and was also very mature for my years with adults. They say that the first five years are the most important bonding years of a child's life, and my early years were simply wonderful. In every area of my life, I lacked nothing and felt second to none. I have so many fantastic memories of those years. They were so splendid full of love, joy, and laughter. I carried them with me all of life, and clung on to them to remember, a time I once had in a time yet to come.

CHAPTER 8

It was a Saturday morning and time for me to get ready to spend the weekend with Aunty Gwen. I was so excited. I loved my weekends at what I called home now, with this newfound family that had welcomed me into their lives a few years ago by now. It came as naturally as night follows day that I would think of them and talk about them as my family. Aunty Gwen and Uncle George were truly the mother and father figures in my life that I had never had, and we fitted like a glove. I learnt so much about normal family life with them.

They had a sixteen-year-old daughter and a fourteen-year-old son and when Aunty Gwen bought her children something, she bought it for me too. When she bought them a new coat or clothing, she always got three items and not two. I had become her little one, her youngest. She never said it but I always knew it. It was such a fun loving fantastic few years with my Aunty Gwen.

I was told many years later that when I first met Uncle George and Aunty Gwen, they had come with the parents of another patient as they were all church friends. But there were too many visitors around the girl's bed so the staff nurse asked would they mind moving from the bed as there should be only two visitors there. As they wondered around the ward Uncle George saw me sitting alone playing with my doll and asked the nurse could they visit me.

'Oh yes,' she'd replied. 'That's Sarah, sadly she has only had a couple of visits in all the years she has been in hospital.'

Uncle George came over with Aunty Gwen to my bed and with a big smile looked down at me chatting and playing away with my doll and said, 'Hello Sarah, may we visit you today?'

It seems I had a huge grin of delight on my little face as I looked up at them saying, 'Oh yes please,' as they pulled a few sweeties out of their pockets for me. I told them to go and get two chairs and sit by my bed like real visitors do and they did. We chatted away and they just loved my little personality. I also said before the end of the visit, 'I don't think I have a Daddy and my Mummy never comes to see me. Will you come to see me and be my Mummy and Daddy?'

It appears they got choked up and I almost broke Aunty Gwen's heart. I made them promise me faithfully they would come and see me on the next visit. After seeing me they went off to the office to see Sister Brendon to get permission to visit me and she told them all about me and my mother. She told them that they could visit as much as they liked but at their own risk if my mother should arrive. Aunty Gwen was to tell me many years later that they both felt at that minute that I was a risk worth taking and they never missed a visit with me after that moment. I can never remember them ever breaking their word or letting me down.

As time passed us all by, I adored my Aunty Gwen and became so attached to her. I can remember her asking Sister Brendon was it possible to have me home over night and bring me back Sunday teatime. Sister Brendon agreed on the condition that someone would take me to mass. Aunty Gwen assured her I would not miss Sunday Church and I never did.

Now Aunty and her family were not Catholics, but they were Christians, and she was a Christian of her word. She got me up on the Sunday Morning and along with Uncle she took me in the car to church. Along the way she told me…

'Listen Sarah, as we promised Sister Brendon, we're taking you to church but it's a bit different from mass. Now we must tell the truth to Sister. You did go to church because you have, but not to say too much about it dear or she won't allow you to stay overnight with us again. We don't want that now do we?'

We certainly didn't. I loved my new family so much and I was clever enough to know what to say and what not to say to make sure I got all the contact I could with them. As we arrived at the little church building and I entered, well I had never seen anything like it in my life. There was a band playing, people singing worship songs banging tambourines and most of the people were clapping, dancing, and singing. There was a pastor which I thought was a priest and I was allowed to think that, so I would call him so in front of Sister Brendon.

Aunty explained that it did not matter what Christian Church I was in, Jesus was there, but many people think Jesus only goes to their church, so we must be careful what we say. People put their hands on each other and prayed and some shouted prayers in this funny language.

I know now it was called praying in the Spirit. It was my first experience of a born-again church which was Pentecostal. It was vibrant, loud, joyous, Spirit filled and exciting and I loved it. I attended it with Aunty and family for a few years after that. Aunty Gwen said I was eight years old when I walked to the front of the Church and gave my heart to Jesus. I do not recall that at although I am sure it happened. Oh, what a blessed and wonderful life I had. I felt I was surely the luckiest child on earth.

Time just trickled by, and all was fine. My eighth birthday had come and gone and thankfully, there was still no sign of that strange lady with the scruffy children bothering me. I felt she must have gone away for ever and didn't seem to worry about her at all anymore. I was in a bubble, and it never once occurred to me it could one day burst, and all would change. I simply thought that this was my life, the way it was mapped out for me, and it was going to stay this way forever.

It was Saturday morning again and I was excited about my usual overnight stay at Aunty Gwen's. I was all dressed and had my tiny weekend case packed sitting on my bed waiting for Uncle George to pick me up at ten o'clock. It was almost ten am and I was watching the windows to see who passed, eager to get off with Uncle George when I suddenly saw someone pass, thinking yippee it was he. You might imagine the shock I got when the door opened and what greeted my eyes left me horrified. *'Oh no!'* I thought. *'Not her again*!' It was the poor lady back again, with a few of those very rude and tatty children. *What was she doing here?*

I started to feel extremely ill-at-ease wondering what she could want. I was sure she would start shouting and saying nasty things to people again and wished that my Uncle George would hurry up and get me out of here, realising almost at once that this was the nasty woman Sister Brendon so easily chose to call my mother. Sister suddenly noticed her from across the ward and hurried over to my mother greeting her with a smile and saying, 'Shall we go into the office Mrs Murphy?' So off they went. Uncle George always picked me up by ten am on Saturdays and I knew it was long past that time, so I asked the nurse exactly what time it was, 'Eleven thirty Sarah,' she replied.

Where is my Uncle George? I thought.

Suddenly Sister Brendon interrupted my thinking and gently took me by the hand and led me silently towards her office. She sat me on the chair and said, 'Sarah your Mummy has come to take you home now. Remember I told you that one day she would?'

I looked at her absolutely full of confusion which was rapidly turning to sheer fear and pleaded, 'Oh no, Sister Brendon, please don't let her take me away!'

'Sarah, my dearest child, I can do nothing. Your Mummy has signed a paper discharging you, which means that you have to go home now and stay with your real Mummy, Daddy, sisters, and brothers. They're your family and they want you back home with them now.'

I jumped up wrapped my arms around her legs and begged in tears, 'But I don't want to go. Please don't make me pleaseee!' I continued to sob as she began to change my clothing, preparing me for leaving. I could see that this was upsetting her as much as me. My Mother entered the office now - she had gone outside for a fag.

'Hey Sally, give your Mammy a hug and a kiss. You're coming home now!' she said in her common Irish accent as she bid me over with a warm coaxing smile, displaying her gummy, empty mouth.

'Thank you but I can't. My Uncle George is coming to collect me soon, isn't he Sister Brendon please tell her?' again I pleaded.

'No Sarah, he is not. You must go with your Mummy today my dear,' Sister Brendon said quietly.

It was hopeless and as my pitiful pleads seemed to fall upon deaf ears, I tried to negotiate a response which might settle me down a bit, 'But it's only for the weekend isn't it?' I looked at them both desperately seeking a yes answer. Sister Brendon lowered her head and turned away from me as my mother said the words that were about to change my life for ever, 'Right Sally come on let's go. You won't be back on Monday; you're coming home forever.' Turning to Sister Brendon she said, 'Sorry Sister, her father wants her home and that's all there is to it, so let's go now, we have buses to catch.'

A knot of panic started to build in my chest, and I sobbed my little heart out as she took my hand and waltzed me through the door out of the hospital and towards the bus stop saying, 'Come on Sally stop that whinging. You're a big girl now. Look, your little sisters are looking at you!'

I sat silently on the long bus ride back home as I sadly came to the realization that my whole world as I knew it had just crumbled in front of me. The very thing that I had always dreaded and feared was happening right now. It seemed nobody could help me, and I could do nothing about it at all. I was to be told many years later that my discharge had been planned for a few days and that was why my Uncle George had not turned up to collect me.

With good intentions Sister Brendon had left it to the last minute to tell me. Firstly, because she wasn't sure if my mother would even turn up - after all she wasn't the most reliable person. Secondly, she wanted to save me as much anxiety as she could. As always, the caring, thoughtful and loving Sister Brendon. *Oh, was I ever going to see her again?* For I knew I was going to miss her awfully. What about all my other friends? There were Rosie and Brenda the nurses, Dr Allen, and Uncle George.

Then there was that beautiful, very kind and loving Christian lady that had taught me in those early years of my life what a true Mother is and how a true Mother loves. She was my Aunty Gwen who for a few years now had taken me under her wing and adored me as her own. To me she was my true Mummy, and we had such an attachment. We had built a huge bond with each other. I had a beautiful closeness with my Aunty Gwen, so much that when I was ripped out of her life, the endless ache in my chest felt like my heart had broken into many pieces. *How was I going to live without her?*

At just eight years old, I had to accept and deal with emotions and feelings of upset and disappointment no child should have to cope with. So as fear gripped tightly to my emotions and confusion flooded my mind, I couldn't help but wonder, *what was in store for me now, and who are these people who say they are my family?*

CHAPTER 9

Arriving home was like stepping into another world. I could not believe what consumed my eyes when we walked into front garden. Rubbish bags spilled everywhere obviously torn open by animals scavenging for food. Broken bits of cheap, plastic toys and old clothing were strewn across the front garden. Weeds, dandelions, and bunches of grass sprouted up from the mud.

I had never seen windows like these in my life; I am sure they'd never been washed. They were filthy, so filthy that they wouldn't have needed curtains, for no-one could see in or out anyway. A couple of the glass panes were missing and replaced with cardboard or a black plastic bin bag. The front door was painted a horrid light green colour, with more paint off it than on.

Now you might think this couldn't get worse, but it did. The letterbox was missing, so they had nailed some cardboard on the inside of the door for the postman to push the mail through, but nobody could see in from the outside. I hadn't even got through the front door yet and I was in the horrors.

On opening the front door, I was absolutely gobsmacked. The place was like a tip with loads of little trampy children running about. The only thing I could relate it to was the film Oliver Twist I had seen. I sort of went into a mild state of shock and could only see what was before me as the voices seemed to fade into the background. While standing at the door scanning the room in sheer disbelief, I felt the sudden presence of a man who to my annoyance smiled and picked me up, (which I did not like at all.) My body went stiff and reacted by drawing back from him as he tried to place a kiss on my cheek, making my discomfort to it all blatant for all to see.

My Mother seeing this said in her usual common Dublin accent, 'Sally it's okay this is your father, now give your Daddy a kiss and hug!'

Give my daddy a kiss and hug? She must be out of her mind! I was just eight years old, and I had never met this man before in my life. He had never made the smallest effort to get to know me and in-fact had abandoned me to a hospital bed. There was no sensitivity what-so-ever to these facts. He put me down rather swiftly. It was apparent he took my rejection of him personally and was offended. It became all about him and I could see he carried great power in this house and people, particularly my mother, tip-toed around him.

It was pretty obvious that they were uneducated, as common as muck and pig ignorant people and sadly raised their children in the same manner. I wasn't like that though. I was spotlessly clean and educated for my years. I could read and write (my mother couldn't even do that) I spoke beautifully and was not afraid to give my opinion. After all, I had been brought up from days before I can remember, being encouraged to express myself. As long as I respected my elders, and spoke it in a polite manner, I'd been taught that it was good for a child to have an opinion.

'She doesn't know ya Paddy, give her some time!' said my mother a little nervously. With that he got his jacket and went off to the pub. I couldn't help but notice the dull, shabby, worn-out, and badly marked ripped wallpaper. The hanging net on the window was unreal and only added more distaste to the cheap, vile fibre-glass curtains. The floorboards were clearly visible under the torn, thin, worn-out vile lino. It had all sorts of spilled drinks over it, lumps of greasy, thick dirt throughout and was covered with rubbish the kids had slung there. It was clear it hadn't been swept or washed for a while. In the corners of the room stood four well used yet old fashioned, manky chairs. While in the centre of the room was a large extremely old-fashioned table, surrounded by my five siblings who stuffed their mouths with anything they could grab. They had no manners at all, I was utterly disgusted and determined I would never eat off such thing.

The table was square and covered with a cheap, nasty plastic tablecloth, which was split and burnt showing a little more table than cloth. It was covered with cracked and chipped cups, a jam jar, a milk bottle half filled with cold tea, a buttered broken-handled knife, half a bottle of milk, and a tablespoon inside an opened bag of sugar. I noticed a silver tea pot all burnt on the bottom from being put on the stove and a small broken handled pot which I think they boiled the baby's milk in. My Mother was putting sugar onto a slice of bread folding it like a sandwich and giving it to the kids who to my amazement were loving it.

There was a large hole on the ceiling surrounded by cobwebs and the ceiling paper draped down, revealing dried, splattered drinks and bits of hard food, which must have been slung at it. From the centre of the cracked, dusty, filthy ceiling overlooking the table, hung a dim, shadeless light bulb, which was switched on. I thought this was quite ridiculous for if they had only cleaned the windows, more light would have got in. Yet even though the light looked so depressive and dull, it still managed to reveal the small, filthy, grimy room at its worst.

A little boy ran about amidst the filth. He could have only been eighteen months or so and was partly dressed. Again, I was stunned at the lack of clothing he wore and the disgusting habits he portrayed, but it didn't stop me liking him. A dirty, shabby, red, tiny, ripped jumper with a hole in the sleeve covered his little chest and no trousers covered his tiny bare bum, and no socks and shoes covered his cute but grubby titchy feet. Although he was filthy with tatty greasy hair, I immediately fell in love with his big brown eyes and gorgeous little face when he smiled at me.

He came running over, and to my horror, mucked on the floor right next to me. Mother grabbed a piece of newspaper, wiped his backside, and picked up the poo with it before throwing it into the plastic rubbish bag which hung on a kitchen cabinet handle. I didn't notice her wash her hands or wash his bum. This clearly added to the stench riddled place anyway. I had truly never ever smelled a place as bad as this in all my life. The smell was so foul it was sickening and a few times I thought I might vomit.

It was a freezing day and yet my two younger sisters wore very little. A thin dress and shabby cardigan covered their little skinny bodies, followed by filthy ankle socks and dirty cheap plastic sandals. They had dry, yet sweaty grimy skin and greasy uncombed hair.

Yet, in spite of this, they were very pretty and cheerful children. Next in line were two little brothers, one was four and the other three. They looked very tatty and unkempt too. The final sibling was the little toddler who had just soiled beside me. It was at this point that I realised I was the first-born child in this family.

How different I was to these pleasant but poor little children. I remember hearing a story about a little matchstick girl who was a pauper. I couldn't help but think these little ones must be real paupers. I thought poor people, tramps and paupers were only in fairy tales. Yet in-spite of the circumstances they really did seem cheerful, lively, and happy enough in their own little world. After all, they knew nothing better. They had been born into this way of life and it was very normal to them. It was me that was strange; they thought I was a posh person.

To these sorts of people, anyone who worked was wealthy. I must have seemed very rich to them, and a great feeling of pity crept through me for their plight. I didn't know what I was going to do, but I truly felt I couldn't stay. This was simply awful, and I didn't fit in at all. It was so different to all I'd ever known. I had just left a clean, warm, caring loving environment.

I looked down at my fine clean clothes and strong, polished boots. I couldn't understand why this way of living didn't seem to bother these people at all. Despite the appalling conditions, they ran about as if they didn't have a care in the world. Obviously because they'd known nothing different and what was crazy to me was normality to them. Yet to me it was a massive blow and a huge shock to the system

I walked to the kitchen to get a glass of water and on my life, it was as if this trail of filth was following me? No way was I drinking in this place. The brick walls were painted a dark ugly yellow and in parts showed splattered refreshments and caked in food stuck to the walls surrounded by thick dust. Far up the wall almost next to the ceiling was a small filthy window consisting of six little panes of glass, which were so thick with grime, the dim kitchen light had to be left on even in the day whilst someone was using the kitchen. Down from the window and expanding from the brick painted wall was a large white grimy square sink with an old dim brass tap (never polished) which was for cold water only. The sink was piled high with dirty old pots, filthy dishes, cups, and broken jam jars.

I could go on forever taking you through all the rooms telling you the same shocking story showing the massive contrasts, from all I had known, to what I now had to learn to accept. I was standing in this dirty hole of squalor and poverty in tears, not knowing which way to turn. Yet back in the front room that lady sister Brendon insisted was my mother, sat in the midst of it all shouting at the younger ones to pack it in, and threatening another as she clutched her bottle of beer and puffed away at a cigarette. A frightened, uneasy feeling crept into the pit of my stomach which slowly began to turn to horror, as I realised that the beautiful, peaceful, loving, and clean world I had known all my life, was gone for ever.

I decided that I would rather die than spend a minute in that place. So, I wondered up the stairs into the bedroom at the top to be alone and pray. There was nothing in it at all, it was completely empty. So, I fell to my knees on the hard floorboards and began to speak to Jesus, 'This can't be true -I must be dreaming and it's a nightmare. Oh, wake me up, wake me up, now, please dear Jesus and let me see my Sister Brendon and Aunty Gwen again.' I was bewildered and full of despair, but deep down I knew. This was no nightmare; it was real, and I was going to have to try to get on with it. I had to become a part of these people and this way of life.

CHAPTER 10

As the weeks flew by, I got to know and like my little brothers and sisters but found it very hard to accept my parents and new home. I often played with my siblings for a while as our parents slung us out of the door to play for a few hours, and us older ones were expected to take care of the nippers. Yet I always seemed to drift off unnoticed and make my way to a private place to talk to what I felt was my only loyal, true, and loving friend - Jesus. I needed to know why I was still here, and why my prayers were not being answered.

I was more than just homesick for my old life. I longed for what I felt was my true family which consisted of Sister Brendon and the Mother I truly longed for - Aunty Gwen. I started to resent Jesus, for I felt he had really let me down and my prayers were falling upon deaf ears. I blamed Him for what I saw as forgetting me and forsaking me in this pit of misery.

In hospital and with Aunty Gwen I was encouraged and helped to read my Bible. The nuns did this wonderfully and without boring us. They would bring the message of God, the meaning of the Bible and the life of Jesus Christ over to us in a way our young minds could understand and accept.

I'd always liked my Bible studies and loved to learn the meanings and messages from God. I was a very religious little girl and found comfort in God. So, I really tried hard to learn the Bible because I was determined that one day, I was going to be a nun like Sister Brendon, and I wanted to know all about God and Jesus for whom I would work.

Religion Instruction, RI as we called it in my school days, was the one subject I never tired of or regretted learning. Yet at this time of my life, I wasn't sure why I had once thought that way. Even though I was very angry with Jesus, I still went on my little walk about when I could to a private spot to speak to Him.

I had only been home a short while before it became obvious to me, that my father was far from a religious man. He said he didn't believe in God; it was a load of 'Bollocks!' I wasn't sure at all what he could have meant by that, but I was beginning to get a pretty clear picture that this man was not a pleasant guy. In fact, he was moody, foul, vulgar mouthed, aggressive and an utterly selfish person. He was self-absorbed to the core and ruled with an iron rod - not in a biblical fashion either.

It was apparent he couldn't digest me and didn't like me at all. My Father often caught me praying and did not like that one bit. He often said that the Nuns had brain washed me and that I was to take no notice of that load of crap anymore. He felt they were all a bunch of hypocrites, and it was time that my nonsense came to a stop. The more he caught me praying over the next few weeks, the less patient he became, displaying an aggravated attitude towards me.

I recall him returning home late one night as pissed as a skunk. I was sleeping with the children, and he woke me saying, 'You know Sally all this about your God is a load of shite and I don't what you filling my kids heads with that f***ing stuff.'

'Paddy, leave her be and come to bed!' I heard.

He ignored Mum and continued saying, 'Did you hear what I said to you Sally?'

'Yes Dad,' I replied nervously.

'What did I say then?' he asked goading me to repeat it.

'You said a very bad thing about Father God Dad!'

'And what very bad thing was that then?' he replied, mimicking me in a very childish mocking fashion.

'You need to stop having an answer for everything when I speak to you; it's about time I started to pull you in line girl,' he went on to say. I felt it better to keep my mouth shut, but I hadn't been rude or cheeky anyway and by now he was really giving me the creeps. My Mother intervened saying, 'Paddy, come on now, let it go you've had too much to drink. Go to bed now come on!'

This appeared to stop him in his tracks, and he got off our bed and walked to Mum's bed informing me that he had had a bellyful of my airs and graces. It was time for me to fall into line with the other kids and as he took off his trousers to get into bed with my mother, he continued to say that I must stop acting the fool for my own sake and give up kneeling down talking to myself. He felt he had enough of my rubbish now and if I did it again, he would class it as a sheer act of disrespect to him and pure disobedience. I didn't know what to think, I didn't know what I had done. This was sheer madness, and while thinking that I seriously considered myself warned.

It didn't take much to notice the fact that my mother was rather keen on the booze too, but in saying that, I guess she was the better of the two. He was just a pure nasty git drunk or sober, and I loathed him, but she was simply pathetic when she had a few to many. Sometimes she might act the opposite way, by stirring father up and goading him until he snapped and went nuts.

I was caught between the river and the deep blue sea and didn't know what way to turn. Not that our feelings mattered at all to these two. As I got older, I realized it was all about them and children weren't always a joy. There were times I had no doubt we were also a huge inconvenience. As strange as it seemed, the attitude of many families from this environment was simply this, the older children were second class citizens, their needs always followed the parents, and they were there to look after and skivvy after the family. It wasn't frowned on much either, after all in wasn't far off the days of child labour when children went down the mines.

Kids should be seen and not heard and after all we we're just 'Kids'. Their attitude was that kids don't understand an adult's world and there was nothing wrong with their drinking. Didn't everybody drink? Trouble was, my siblings may not have noticed and known what was going on, they had been born into it and this was a normal life to them, but not for me. I understood perfectly well that there was something disturbing about my parents and that something very wrong was happening in this house.

I don't know how long I had been home when our parents started to go out more and more leaving me in charge of the house and the little ones. So often we siblings sat all hugged together, discussing the events of their previous drink just a few days before. At times my brother or sister would mimic their behaviours including trying to copy Mum's Irish accident and vile language, seeing that they always seemed to fall out and fight when they were drunk.

Yet watching my younger siblings acting out the disgraceful manner in which they returned home, was so funny - most likely one of the few times I laughed from the heart at this point of my childhood. Yes for a while we all forgot our troubles and giggled our socks off, but getting near the time of their return (if they returned that night at all) we all got a little quiet and truth be known, somewhat anxious for we dreaded and hated what was sure to come.

I despised my life and every day the nightmare got worse. I had been dragged unwillingly into a filthy, depraved, terror-filled sordid, dark, and claustrophobic world.

This was the Birmingham slums in the early 1960s, and life was harsh for those who lived there. It was a merciless environment overflowing with people on the breadline. Many were decent, hardworking families that simply worked in low paid jobs so couldn't afford to live anywhere but low paying housing, which sadly for them meant the ghettos. So, they had to put up living next door to families such has ours. Others did what they had to do for their survival. So, in short, the slums were mostly made up of alcoholics, drug addicts, criminals and all sorts of immigrants.

This area horded the vilest of the vile, that drank far too much and boasted of their mischiefs. They were truly the meanest spirited people I knew with no regard for people, property, or life. They robbed anybody, even their own. They fought with anybody, even their own, and in their many drunken brawls, often battered, bottled, stabbed, wounded, or even killed, anybody, even their own. Talk about no place for a child.

Many kids grew up believing school didn't matter, that it was okay to get drunk and batter your wife or family that crime pays and never be polite or nice to the police for they were our enemies and to trust them, talk to them or tell them anything was to be a grass and a grass might be severely dealt with in this world.

This was so hard for me to understand. I liked the police officers. I'd always believed that they were good people who protect us. I wasn't sure I could be rude to them. After all, Uncle Bob was a policeman, and he was lovely. Oh, everything I had ever been taught was being contradicted and I was very confused with it all. Deep in my heart I felt a great shame and utter disgust with my parents and their chosen way of life. Although I pitied my mother at times, I still couldn't help but think, that for a mother, her behaviour was outrageous.

Well, I mean, even living in a disgraceful place such as this, it was not seen as an acceptable excuse to live like or behave like animals. In short, we may have lived in a sty, but we didn't have to behave like pigs. There was a code of conduct expected of all. Even in the ghettos a woman was expected to behave in an appropriate manner. She was to keep a low profile, keep her business to herself, keep her home in order, and stand by her man. Well, that's how the decent families conducted themselves, but families like mine were as disruptive as they could be and loved an audience when acting like tough guys.

They spent their time drunk, intimidating people into a wall of silence so the neighbours would fear calling the police regardless to what they heard or saw. If anyone disagreed or dared to stand their ground and defy my father, they got battered by him or the criminal thugs he brought around. They portrayed themselves as a good, loving, large Irish family that took great pride in bringing up their many children.

Now this is one of the reasons I called them pig ignorant. It never occurred to them for one minute that this was deluded thinking. They actually believed their own lies, but others saw straight through it. People could see the state of the place and the state of the children. They could hear my parents returning home pissed more than not. They heard the cries and screams in the night when he was in a drunken rage and battering his wife. I knew who the real hypocrite was here, and it wasn't Sister Brendon as he often said. This house was built on a pillow of lies and was in the grip of a destructive force. It was ruled by a domineering, callous overpowering drunken bully. I knew we were being pushed down a very rocky pathway and I feared for our future.

CHAPTER 11

I recognised the drunken singing voice of my mother as my parents returning from a night on the booze made their way home. It must have been around eleven thirty and I could hear the steel caps of my father's shoes as he carried my mother towards the back entry. I felt really uneasy as I heard them coming into the back yard and on entering the house, he dropped Mum into a chair and got my little sister up off the settee telling her to go to bed. I tried to follow but was stopped in my tracks, 'Hang on there you – where do you think you're going?

'To bed Dad,' I replied, beginning to feel sick in my stomach knowing he was about to start. I hadn't got a clue what had made him angry, but what I did know was, I was for it again this night.

I cannot remember when I first became the subject of his violence, but I know it wasn't too long after my departure from the hospital. I had been given new names by my father - these names were my nick names I was told. I had eczema and often suffered very badly with it those days. Obviously due to stress, dust, and filth my skin was badly irritated, plus my ointments which I should have had on twice a day had never been put on since leaving hospital. In fact, I had never seen a doctor since then either.

At St Gerald's I can never remember suffering with my eczema like this because it was nursed and under control. However due to this awful skin condition I was called 'Scabby' and due to the fact that I also had disabilities, at times, depending on his spiteful moods, I was either called Scabby or Peg-leg. Mum was still unconscious in a drunken heap while I was left to the mercy of this cold-hearted character.

'Well, Madam Muck, get over here. You hate me, don't you?' he said sitting in his chair, all powerful like a true King of his domain, Captain of his ship, a legend in his own mind. He started bidding me over with his finger, giving me a nasty look and I began shaking from the top of my head to the soles of my feet as I slowly walked towards him.

'No Daddy, I don't, really,' I pleaded, sensing that something bad was about to happen. I did hate him, and he knew it, but I was too scared to admit it.

'Do you like me, Scab?'

'Yes Daddy,' I replied, by now petrified.

'You f****** liar!' he snarled. 'You hate me, you little bastard! Tell the truth. I see you're a gutless little coward!'

Suddenly my mother stirred, 'Stop it Paddy for F***-sake – if it's not me getting digs it's her! Give us a break – Sally, go up the stairs now!' she said.

'Don't move Scab!' he warned.

I froze on the spot as he walked over and punched Mum straight in the face, knocking her into limbo, leaving her lying on the ground covered in blood. He turned and came towards me. By now the kids were screaming and pleading with Dad to stop from the top of the stairs.

'She isn't moving, now to deal with you,' he snarled.

I stood, glued to the floor, fear keeping me paralysed. I just couldn't move.

'I hate you – I hate everything about you - you're not mine you little spastic.'

As he said that my father suddenly slapped me forcefully across the face, knocking me to the floor so I ended up lying with my mother. I woke to a massive bump on my head where I had hit the ground and a welted red mark on my face.

Suddenly I heard, 'You cheeky Bastard – you're saying she's not yours! Oh, she's yours alright – you bleedin' forced yourself on me you f***ing arsehole and well you know it!'

It was my mother who had just come too again. I was unsure whether this verbal attack on him was a mother's care for her battered child, or a reaction to what she had just heard. For if I didn't belong to him, then he was suggesting she must have slept with another. To be honest as sad as this fact is, I think the thought of him suggesting she slept with someone else was the problem here.

'Force myself on you? What a load of shite! I didn't have to - bleeding yo-yo knickers!'

This was far from the truth, and he knew it deep down. He often referred to it on a good day. She was very naive and innocent when he met her.

'Yo-yo knickers, you called your own wife a whore in front of your daughter! I hate your guts, Paddy! You're the biggest diabolical Bastard on two feet!'

Oh no why did she have to bring me into it? I thought, still pretending to be conked out. Even though I was terrified, this seemed the safest thing to do at the minute if I could just hold my nerve. There was always the possibility that he might get exhausted, go to bed, and fall into a drunken sleep, but no such luck for that at the minute, he was bursting with rage and determined to vent it on his chosen victims of the night. Which was always me these days and sometimes Mum.

'You illiterate dummy, you couldn't even boil an egg when we met, you f***ing retard!' shouted my father in a rage grabbing hold of her and raining blows on her that seemed endless.

I was still lying on the ground in a state of shock, pretending to be asleep in the hope that he would leave me alone this night. Fear pumped through my body as I silently prayed that God would hide me from him, and he wouldn't notice me again. When to my horror I suddenly heard myself scream, 'No Daddy, please don't hit her again. Please don't, her nose is bleeding.'

Turning to me he sneered, 'You little scabby bastard, look at you! You're just like her. Can you still pray girl? Well pray to your Jesus for her now and believe me Scab, not even he'll save the whore that bore you tonight.'

Then, turning his attentions to me, he pulled me by the hair and slapped me sharply across the face several times before throwing me to the ground and kicking me sharply away from him like a dog. Oh, I couldn't breathe for a few seconds – the pain being so strong I felt sick, and I rolled around the floor in agony.

'F*** it,' he said as he walked out of the room and up the stairs. 'Bed, now,' he told the other kids, leaving my mother and I bleeding, black and blue lying on the lino of a cold living room.

I stayed there until dawn, too afraid to go up the stairs. I cuddled into Mum, who I knew wasn't dead because I could hear her deep drunken snoring. It wasn't that I loved her that made me hug her. We had both gone through the mill that night. We had both taken a merciless beating and were left lying in our own blood on the floor wounded. Battered and bruised with a swollen face, sore head, and painful body I lay close to her shaking and silently sobbing.

My life had turned from joy to sheer terror, and regardless to how much I racked my brain for a solution there was simply no-way out, nowhere to go and no one to turn to. I must have dozed off to sleep because I woke to the sound of someone choking, as if they were having trouble breathing. I realized it was Mum so I bent closer to look properly and could see that the blood up her nose and in her mouth was blocking her airways. I gently put her head down again and quickly went to the kitchen to warm some water.

I waited quietly for it to warm on the stove and put some coats over her to keep her warm, sneaking about and praying that my father wouldn't wake up again. I shuddered at the thought of what might happen if he did.

It didn't take long for the water to heat so I got a piece of rag, put it under my arm and carried the pot into where my mother lay. Once again, I knelt down beside her and began to wash the blood from her mouth and nose. That at least seemed to help her breathe much better. I then gently began to bathe her face and the more I bathed the more upset I became at the horror the past nights events had left behind. She had cuts, bruising and swelling as well as the two biggest black eyes I'd ever seen.

I had never seen anything like this in my life. When finished, I pushed the pot to one side and began to gently stroke her head. The more I looked at this poor, battered, broken woman, the more moved I became until tears flowed from my eyes. I sat there cradling her head and prayed to Jesus, the only friend that I had whom I trusted, 'Oh Jesus, please stop my Father doing these things. Will you also make sure that my mother wakes up and when you make it all right, then get me out of here please Lord.'

After a while I tried to wake my mother so we could now go to bed and have a few hours' sleep before I had to get up with the children, but she would not wake. I knew it was safe to go up to bed now because he was in a deep sleep and would be too lazy to get out of bed to even hit us now. For heaven's sake there must have been about 15 milk bottles of stale urine in the room because he was too lazy to go out to the toilet. Plus, there was always a bucket full of pee and poo in the room too. It never got emptied for days so you can well imagine the stink coming from that as well. By now all of us were so used to it we couldn't smell it at all. We got used to literally lying in piss and shit.

But seeing that my mother wasn't moving this night, I cuddled up beside her on the floor. I was determined not to leave her alone but hoped that I might get enough sleep for I knew that once the kids woke up, I had to get up and take care of them while Mum went off up to bed.

It was more than obvious that my father had serious issues with me. He could not stand me. I would hear him telling Mum and his friends, 'I just can't take to her - I can't stand her.'

I heard his friend reply once, 'It's not her fault Paddy – she's just a kid and has been raised different. Give her time - it will take time to bond with her.'

'Jimmy, I could be around her 100 years, and I'll still feel the same, there's just something about that kid I cannot take too!'

This man my mother called my father was the most disgusting human being I had ever met in my young years of life. He was selfish, lazy, a drunkard, a wife beater and child abuser. A whore master, a bully, vulgar and I am sure so very much more. I only ever saw him working once, which only lasted a few weeks. His usual routine was to sleep in bed, and when he woke up, we took him up a cup of tea and the Daily Mirror. I dreaded taking the tea up but most of the time had to.

He rarely passed any remarks to the evidence he had left behind from the previous night when he'd beaten the crap out of me. Apart from, 'You won't be going to school for a few weeks.' When he decided to come down the stairs and show his face, he'd lie on the settee and again Mum or me, and it was usually me, ended up skivvying after him until he went out drinking.

He was my Father whether he wanted to be or not and the Father of all these children. By now Mum was having babies almost every eleven months. Although I liked new babies and as sweet as they were they were never a blessing to me. For it was just another responsibility and more work for my half-starved, undernourished, weary little mind and body to cope with. As time passed, I couldn't help but wonder why my mother put up with it. Why did she not just grab her children and leave? I used to think that she was as bad as him, allowing her children to be put through these terrifying ordeals time after time.

I couldn't understand for the life of me why she would keep allowing this to happen to them and to us. He wasn't beating his other children. In fact, he loved the others and was pretty good to them in many ways, and they deeply loved him, but to keep beating up his wife or me, was too much for them. They dreaded the violence; it was terrifying for them and they went through hours of awful panic and distress on these occasions. No, I couldn't make it out at all. What on earth was in this woman's mind that she didn't even attempt to get us all out of there.

CHAPTER 12

The fear and stress of my life was affecting my health by now. I scratched my skin continuously. Even though I knew I was going to get severely beaten for it, I simply could not stop. The huge scabs behind my ears, knees and arms were now spreading around my body rapidly. The sores began festering in places causing a serious infection in other parts of my body which left a sticky, itchy, leaking puss that stuck to my clothes and to my skin making it very painful indeed.

It didn't help at all lying on a bare mattress and being covered in dirty old blankets and coats each night. That only irritated my skin complaint even more. My parents, being as ignorant hillbilly's, still talked as though they knew everything, but had no understanding of this skin disease at all.

There was a possibility that they didn't realise that their behaviour, plus the filth and all the stress, did not help the problem in the slightest, but added greatly to this condition. More to the point though, the facts were showing that they really didn't care at all. The itching almost drove me mad and the more I tried to stop, the worse it got. I couldn't control this at all without treatment. I needed tablets, cream and by now, daily dressings.

However, my parents being as thick as muck and twice as sloppy, naturally thought that they knew best, and saw my endless scratching as my fault for being dirty. They felt the fact that I persisted to scratch was in sheer defiance of them. In their eyes, I would scratch until I bled to attract attention to myself, because I was looking for sympathy, and my father felt it was badness on my behalf.

I tip toed around my dad for I had never been comfortable with him. I disliked him immensely and feared him terribly. Being so different in my manner, my attitude, and behaviours from the rest of his children, and he not having that chance to get to know me from infancy as he did the other siblings, meant that there was no bonding between us due to his absence in my early years. I guess now I can understand the struggle it all must have been for him. In short, he was living with a child stranger of whom he couldn't take to. Although this house and their way of living was very questionable, it was all they knew and seemed to suit them. But it wasn't all I knew, and it certainly didn't suit me.

My very presence and unintentional demeanour showed him how very different things should be in the home and this only added to the endless feelings of guilt he carried. He drowned his sorrows with drink, but we had to face our sorrows head on with nothing to desensitize us and ease the pain or fear.

The more I disliked him the more I tried to keep out of his way if I could but there was no-where to hide from this man. Unlike his other kids he was very abrupt with me even when trying to be playful and that was a real rarity in my case. Just to be included in their fun or be allowed to play their games was simply thrilling but never lasted long. I had to learn to grow up quick in the place, so just to be allowed to be my age and act my age was such a blessing even though short lived. It ended as usual, with Father being unable to keep up the charade of false kindness towards me and so every game always ended with him mocking me and making a laughingstock of me. He often invited my siblings to participate and them thinking it a game in so finding it funny would join in. It was just another nail in my emotional coffin leaving me feeling even more deflated and even more unwanted!

Mother did try and clean the house when she was off the drink, but it was mainly left to me and my younger sister. Being the little lovable rogue of the family, she would help a little then bugger off, leaving most of the work for me to do for she knew I would do it. I dared not do the work for fear of a beating. At times I resented her for that but not for long, as deep in my heart I adored her. I knew and understood her cheeky, loveable, pleasant spirit, and her being just her helped me so much in so many ways when I felt hurt, sad, and lonely.

It was obvious at this stage that my father could not accept me and had even given up the will to try. I had to get streetwise and quick to try and silently outwit this guy in my will to survive. Being forward for my years not to say on the ball, I began to read him like a book. I knew only too well that drunk or dry my father hated the sight of me. The more he drank the worse his behaviour got, until his beatings came so often, I didn't know if I was coming or going. And it wasn't just me. The beauty that had once radiated from my young Mother's face was now a mass of scars, thread-veins, and endless worry lines. Then at other times Dad would beat me so badly that I had to spend months out of school.

There were times when Mum had bouts of time on the drink. She would get drunk with Dad as much as she could. A huge chunk of the much-needed social security money went on booze or repaying borrowed money for drink the week before. Being alcoholics, you can imagine the never-ending penny pinching that went on. Continually robbing Peter to Pay Paul. So many a time we went without food for a day or so.

While Mum was in these phases of her life, the burden of housework seemed to fall on me. I alone was responsible for the house and caring for the children. I had to clean up, get the children to school, feed them and wash them and wore-be-tide me if it wasn't done. If and when I was lucky enough to attend school, when I returned home for the lunch hour with my sibling (to receive at least three days out of five, just a plate of watery mixed corn flour or a few biscuits, before returning to school) my Father would look at me and say, 'If the teacher asks - what did you have for lunch, what will you say Sally?'

'Chicken, roast potatoes, mash potatoes and gravy, Dad,' I replied.

'And don't forget it, or you'll be sorry!' he threatened. 'Keep your eye on her at school,' he often said to my sister. In other words, make sure she does not talk to the teachers alone.

You wouldn't think this could get any worse than it already was, but it did. Our situation deteriorated day by the day. The neglect was ridiculous and the abuse outrageous and we were helpless and powerless to do anything about it at all. I hardly went to school when my parents were on their drinking sprees. I only spoke when spoken to which was rarely at all as nobody was allowed to speak to me a lot of the time these days. My beautiful little brothers and sisters often broke Dad's law and gave me a quick hug or kiss at their own risk. If Dad was in one of his crazy moods, I wasn't even allowed in the same room as my siblings. I was only demanded in there in the most terrifying situations which was to receive even more physical punishment for doing nothing wrong at all - except for being born. I came to learn the true meaning of loneliness, and to be careful who I trusted even amongst my younger brothers and sisters.

I knew hard work, I knew how to take a beating, and I knew responsibility. Regardless to how nice Mum tried to be when Dad wasn't around, I knew not to trust her and keep my mouth shut, which for me was a no-win situation. Saying nothing about anything, to her was seen as ignoring her. Yet answering her as she chatted away about Dad and the way he treated her was interpreted as slagging him off. Either way I was for it. I began to wish that I hadn't been born. So often she told unnecessary tales about me which always ended up with me at the vile end of another beating. I couldn't understand at all why she did this. After-all she knew only too well what it was like to be in his bad books.

I was mortified as she would suddenly turn on me when she returned from the pub and began stirring him up about things I had said (which she started) so his focus and his need for violence and blood turned my way more than not. Thinking back on it all now I came to realize and understand her. It was sad for her really. She'd been trapped in a violent marriage for years with loads of children and could not see a way out of this life that she had come to dread so much. I don't think she could cope with another beating. She was terrified and had no-where to go herself, never mind dragging a load of children along. In those days there was no such thing as a refuge for battered women and the police could do very little, so very little was done about domestic violence at that time. So, for me as a little girl I felt surrounded by turncoats and was left alone to cope and find a way to get away from my daily plight.

I recall one of the nights after Mum had finished shit-stirring to Dad about me, he told her to leave the room and take the kids to bed. Oh my, I absolutely crapped myself; I knew I was in serious trouble this time. He had a look on his face that sent chills up my spine and the most awful thing about this is that you can't run, there's nowhere to hide, and no-one to save you. What was coming was coming and there was nothing I could do about it apart from accepting the horrors before me.

As soon as she'd closed the front room door, he swung round and punched me in the stomach with such force I flew across the room and landed in a heap on the floor. I doubled up in pain, gasping for breath as a burning, ripping pain soared through my body, bursting out of my throat until I almost choked. Still furious, my father flew over to me and at the sight of me screaming doubled up on the floor, without a sign of mercy; he sharply booted me in my crippled leg. I rolled over in even more agony, clutching that painful part of my body and cried out endlessly in fear and pain pleading with him to stop between my pitiful sobs. But with no time to recover he pulled me to my feet by my hair and punched me to my face which burst my eyebrow, my nose and mouth in one go then he dropped me to the floor like a rag doll.

My vision went blurred - I could feel no pain and for a moment all about me seemed to go blank. Opening my eyes I saw my mother crawling towards me, screaming, 'No Paddy No!'

I looked up to see the large mad eyes of my Father as he put his hands over my nose and mouth and pressed them down on my face so I couldn't breathe. I struggled in panic, rapidly moving my head, desperately searching for air but it was useless. I could not be freed and at that point became frozen with fear and realized that I was in a struggle for my very life. My father was attempting to murder me, and I couldn't do anything about it at all.

I was surely now about to die and maybe this wouldn't be such a bad thing because now, at last, all my pain would stop. My face felt bloated as a tightening pain gripped my chest. My eyes felt like they would pop out of my face, and I thought my lungs were about to burst. Even though I knew it would bring relief I decided I did not want to die and just knowing I was about to was worse than anything I had ever suffered. I was weak and there was no more fight left in me, so I began to pray to Jesus to bring me to heaven quickly and stop this torture for ever.

Then everything went black.

Merciful Jesus what am I doing, I almost killed her,' he knelt beside me and lifted my battered little head onto his knee. My weak limp little body just lay there. He began to sob stroking my hair back gently, 'Sally I'm sorry, I don't mean to do these things to you, you're only a kid.' He was sobbing. This tenderness was a rarity, but I also knew it wouldn't last and he would beat me again. But for a few days I would be free of that and for now I could relax for a short while and drink in these short-lived acts of kindness.

He carried me to the settee and told Mum to get something to put under my head and a blanket. While she did that, he got some warm water and started bathing my face to wash the blood off and assess the damage. Then he covered me on the settee telling me to sleep.

I could hear him talking to my mother saying, 'Oh God look what I've done, you need to get me stopped. Just look what I've done to her! Stop me before I kill her. You're her mother. You have to have me stopped, please!'

There was a genuine tone in his voice that I hadn't heard before. He continued to plead with my mother, 'You need to listen to me now and I am being serious, please put an end to all this. I don't feel I can. I can't control myself when I get like that. So go now and get the cops, get them in to get me out before it's too late and I do something regretful to Sally. Destroy me now, I beg you, before I destroy her!'

This wasn't the first time I'd heard him beg Mum to help him stop in these moments of guilt he had after he'd given me a beating, but Mum never listened.

'I can't Paddy,' she replied sobbing. 'I love you. That's why I stay; I'd sooner suffer your beatings than be without you. Your right though, she's too little to keep coping with much more of it.'

'I know, I think you need to get a doctor or an ambulance. Get someone to take her to the hospital; she needs to be looked at to be sure she is okay.'
'I can't Paddy. They'll want to know who did this to her. They'll charge you with GBH or attempted murder. They'll put you away for years if I get help Paddy. We'll have to look after her ourselves. Look she'll be alright leave it to me I'll look after her.'

I really felt a great pity for my dad at this moment and somewhat angry towards my mother. He had presented her with the perfect opportunity to put an end to our terrifying lives, to get him out of the way so he could never hurt us again, and she said no. In-spite of my injuries she refused to have him removed and give us a much-needed break, our chance to heal and live a life without fear. I couldn't believe her and was unsure if I would ever forgive her again.

CHAPTER 13

The guilt from that particular beating must have been quite something because my father actually stayed in for a while after that night and actually tried to stop drinking and be nice to me - for a few months anyway. It was a bit easier to live him when he stopped drinking, but it never lasted for long. Dad went back to drinking just as we all began to relax around the place a bit.

It wasn't long after that Aunty Gwen came to visit me. My Mother went to the door and whispered to Uncle George and Aunty Gwen that I couldn't see them, and it would be best if they left quickly. When I realised Aunty Gwen was there my heart filled with joy. I wanted to run to her and hug her for ever. But I knew better than that - if I did my life wouldn't be worth living after they had left. So, I stood aside, kept my cool and tried to be brave as I fought back the tears.

'Yep, what do you want?' my father said abruptly as he went to the door.

'We have brought Sarah's toys over for her,' Aunty Gwen answered.

'Right, leave them in the front garden then you can go,' he said coolly, eyeing her suspiciously.

'Mr Murphy, can we speak to Sarah for a minute, please?' Uncle George asked nicely.

'No chance, leave the things then get on your bike,' he said rudely.

'Please just a quick hello Mr Murphy?' pleaded Uncle George as I looked on helplessly. A part of me longed to see them but another part wished they would just go because this was going to be bad for me, I was sure. I longed to see them both and felt gutted I couldn't but knew to be open with how I felt would have been risky, for Dad would have surely harmed me.

'Sally come here!' Dad said. As I walked to the door, he put his hand one my shoulder which meant walk no further. I looked at Uncle and Aunty Gwen seriously, too afraid to smile. They smiled at me sweetly holding their arms out for a hug and saying, 'Hello Sarah!'
'Hello,' I replied unmoving. Rejecting their hug and not moving was killing me. I so wanted to run to Aunty Gwen hug her and never let her go and beg her to take me home and never bring me back, but I just stood there.

Shortly after Aunty Gwen left, my heart sank as I fought back the tears of anguish. A lump gripped my throat for I was not sure if I would see these loving people ever again. My toys filled the front garden, and the children took a special interest in them, even the boys. They were all running about from toy to toy screaming with excitement as they played. Shortly after, Mum and Dad went out. They had only been gone a short time before they returned with a guy who gave them some money and took all my toys away.

A few days later whilst walking down the road to get Mum two bottles of milk and sugar from the shop, I suddenly saw all my toys sitting nicely in a second-hand shop window. I stood at the window just glaring at them as tears flowed down my face. I could not understand for the life of me why these people could do all the spiteful, cruel, and awful things to me, or what I had ever done to deserve it.

Shortly after that a uniformed lady started to visit the house. I didn't know who she was at first but later found out she was from the NSPCC. She started to visit us a lot and ask my mother a lot of questions about us children. I noticed that every time she knocked at the door my father hid in the house. I couldn't understand why. She arrived whenever she felt like it and that wasn't from 9am to 5pm either. She arrived in late evenings sometimes and my father would hide me so that the NSPCC officer couldn't see my marks.

She always wanted to know where I was. Mum said in Ireland with my grandmother. After a couple of times the officer asked her for my Grandparent's full address. Mother was so on the spot, she said she couldn't remember, but she was told that she would be back within a day or two and needed some proof of my whereabouts. When she came back, I was present and she often told Mother she would like to speak to me alone, which couldn't be refused. Yet I knew better than to ever say what was going on. If I had been reassured that I would have been removed from the house immediately, I would have spilt the beans on everything, but I knew it was different in those days. If I had told her she would have confronted Mum, then had to get a warrant to take us to the children's family court to be taken into care and made a ward of state. Now I wonder what would have happened to Sally left alone in this house while all this was happening. So, I continued to deny abuse in the house hoping that she would find it.

One evening Father was pissed up to his eyeballs and continuing his barbaric acts of mental and physical abuse towards me. This night he balanced a sweeping brush on the ground, laid me across it and made it spin. This game he played for the children and his own amusement terrified me. My heart pounded so fast I thought I might have a heart attack. While he was well into his little party games to my horror and his bursts of laughter, there was a huge bang on the door. Mother ran in to the kitchen, 'Paddy quick it's that ole one from the NSPYC!' she said meaning NSPCC.

'Scab you know the rules, keep your f***ing mouth shut; otherwise, they'll never save ya before I get ya!' he warned putting me down rapidly before hiding.

The door was opened and in she came. She focused on me, because she knew something was very wrong but without proof, she could really do little.

The NSPCC also got the Social Services involved. It was apparent that they were on to it, yet I was still living through it. Every time these people tried to speak to me alone, I got into even more trouble when they had gone.

Even though I said nothing at all, the fact they had a bit more interest in me infuriated my father, which again wasn't my fault. It was his own fault, and his own guilt that was causing such conflict inside him, coupled with the fear that his time was running out. He knew that if he continued, his days numbered to a huge prison sentence. That is if I lived to tell the tale where many, many died.

The Social Services began arriving at my school. They had me called out of class and began asking questions. Oh-gosh, this was even more trouble for me because one of my siblings was sure to tell that I had been called out of class to talk to someone. I recall the Social Worker asking me, 'Sarah, were did you get these bruises? How did that mark happen? Do you mind letting me see your back and tummy? Please tell me what is happening in your house Sally, I can help you – did your Daddy do this to you dear? We know he lives there?'

I gave my rehearsed answers, 'No it was my brothers and sisters. When we have a fight, they beat me. No Daddy does not live at home truly – I must go back to class – I must go back to class!' I began to get quite stressed and so I was returned to my class. Oh, how I wanted to be brave enough to tell her, let it all out and tell her everything, but I just couldn't.

I often felt that these ladies were complete idiots and did more harm than good when it came to me. I had more beatings through them coming to our house than I can remember. Apparently, I was bad luck, and they never troubled the family before I arrived home. Good old Dad and Mum always apportioning blame, never accepting responsibility.

I think that the one thing that stood out in my mind mostly was Mum telling me once, 'If a man calls and asks for your dad, you must say he doesn't live here, do you hear Sally?' I found out later that the man was from the Social Security and Mum was claiming money for just her and the kids, saying my father had deserted her, so he must not be caught in our home. Strange really that I was brought up from a baby and told I must never lie, yet in this house it seemed I must never tell the truth.

By now, to quote me as a battered child was an understatement. My hair was dull, very thin, and tatty, my leg caused me endless pain and my skin was in an appalling condition almost like a burn victim. I was under-weight and always tired suffering from exhaustion. Not to say my nerves were shattered.

Much of my reoccurring ill-heath was obviously related to the endless torment and stress I was trying to cope with, yet nothing eased up in the home and in-fact my father's behaviour became even more unpredictable and sadistic. A time had come now where there was no time-out or respite from the abuse. I didn't know what to expect on his return from the pubs.

He returned one night and headed straight to the bedroom carrying the sweeping brush. As I heard him coming, I sat up sharply in bed knowing only too well it was me he was coming for again. The fear of God went through my system as sweat rolled down my forehead and my hands started to shake. Then that gut wrenching fear coursed through my system until I felt like vomiting. Dad just stood looking at me for a moment with the usual hateful look on his face. After a moment he said, 'Look at your skin Scabby.' He told me to take my dress off and then got the rough bristled hard yard brush and painfully swept it along my back on my eczema, at the back of my knees and wherever he could. Oh, it hurt so much, and my skin began to bleed and weep.

'You want to scratch Scabby, well let's scratch you then! Reefing your skin like this and bringing trouble on your mother, you know what you're doing you bad little bastard.'
I was in a no-win situation and my hate for this man was growing by the minute. I wished with all my heart he would die if that's what it would take to get him out of my life. I pictured myself stabbing him in the back as he slept and as if reading my mind he said, 'You hate me don't you Scabby?'

'Yes, YES, I do,' I said defiantly. It was as though my mouth had gone mad and spoke without catching my brain. I think I had come to a stage where I couldn't take anymore and just didn't care. I was also hoping for my own death more and more. Anything must be better than this; this wasn't a life worth living. I didn't know if I could cope with another day of fear - another moment of terror. I just thought, *sod it, you vile pig, do your worst. I'm sick to death.*

I was the most helpful and obedient child in the house. Regardless to what I did I was his battering ram. I didn't think. I was just something to kick ten kinds of shit out of. I mattered to very few except my little siblings.

'You're thinking of killing me, aren't you Scab?' he said interrupting my thoughts. This threw me off balance. *How could he know?*

'Pardon Dad?' I stammered.

'You heard. You want to kill me don't you Scab?'
'Dad I just don't want to be hurt anymore!'

'Well, Scabby Sally, listen while I tell you how to go about getting shut of me,' he said like a teacher in front of a class. 'Firstly, you wait until I'm sound asleep. Then you stick a knife as hard as you can into my back and don't forget to twist it Scab and rip it around in my back. When you get the guts to do it, do it good Scab. Rip me up and do the job right, otherwise you're finished and you're dead Scab. Now you do it, get the guts and do it to me, kill be girl before I kill you.'

I began to wonder if I was losing my mind. Was there no end to this man and his madness! My father was an alcoholic, a drunk. After our nights of chaotic havoc with him, he dreaded to wake the next morning and see what he had done the night before. Often, he couldn't look Mum or me in the face. He would get up after his last night's drink, feeling like hell, trembling, fearful, feeling sick and loathing the horror tormenting his mind, as the guilt spread through his system.

'Christ what have I done?' he would groan. 'Not again.' He felt that nothing but another drink would end what he was feeling, yet another drink put him on a merry-go-round of never stopping. So, it became the same old story day after day. When Mum confronted him with what he had done and the facts being he could actually see the damage he had left behind, to my shock he denied it was him.

My Mother often liked a drink herself. She most likely felt if you can't beat them join them, and I am sure simply as a comfort and way out of her fearful life and misery, she now turned to the bottle for her own way out. I guess it was better for her to get pissed, it was her sedation so at least she stopped feeling the blows.

CHAPTER 14

There was a battle raging within me. I struggled with so many confusing feelings, particularly concerning my father. A part of me felt sorry for him but that was always overshadowed by the disgust and dislike I felt; when I remembered the physical and mental abuse I endlessly endured. So many times, I lay in bed and thought of different ways of ending it all. I didn't want to live but I was too scared to die.

It got to the point where I felt enough was enough, so I decided I had suffered enough, and after thinking on it a little more, I decided to run away and took the risk of talking my younger sister into doing it with me.

I made her all sorts of wild promises, like we would have a lovely home and lots of our own toys, loads of sweets and ice cream, and she wouldn't hear Dad bashing Mum or me up again.

I told her we would never be afraid again because I knew the best Mummy in the world who would have her and make us her little girls. She agreed and so we woke early the next morning broke into the back of the TV, stole the money out of it and run away. The youngest child was awake, so I dressed him and brought him with us.

Thank God for small blessings, the physical abuse had not spread to my other siblings. Yes, they got a clout now and again but never battered, Dad adored his other kids. I don't think I could cope with the mental strain of seeing my brothers and sisters being abused. They were as common as muck, as rough as rough, but the most lovable little rouges to be born, and together we all looked like we had just stepped out of the Charles Dickens novel Oliver Twist.

We quickly sneaked out of the house and up the road and then ran and ran until we had gone past a few bus stops, in the hope that we could catch a bus there and nobody would recognize us. Adrenaline pumped through my veins as we jumped on a bus. I started telling the kids that we wouldn't ever have to go back to that house again. I told them that where we were going now, we would have ice cream, jellies, and all lovely things like that.

I don't know how to this day but somehow, we found our way to Aunty Gwen's. As she opened the door, she fell to her knees hugging me and burst into tears. Uncle George also knelt and picked up my baby brother and they both hugged my sister as well.

Unaware of the seriousness of our circumstances, the children and I were overjoyed. Aunty Gwen knowing I had a sweet tooth was giving us all the goodies we desired, and we rejoiced at our newfound freedom, our new house and they liked their new Mummy. However, the realization soon dawned when it became apparent that we would have to go home. As much as Aunty Gwen and Uncle George wanted to keep us, the law wouldn't allow it. So, Uncle George went to inform the police where we were while Aunty Gwen gently told us that we had to return home.

Our moods dropped at once to panic, and we begged her. She wasn't stupid, they had suspected what was happening in our home and now they had the confirmation. It broke their hearts to have to send us back, not for the want of trying, but they were utterly powerless to stop the outcome and we were soon returned home.

All too soon, we were back at Mums. Dad was waiting to greet us of course. He had the kids put to bed then called me and my sister over, 'Okay what happened?' he said. I could tell by the tone in his voice and the expression on his face that I was in for some beating tonight. Quickly my sister decided to lie, 'Oh, those people Sally knew from the hospital came in a car and asked us to go for a ride with them, didn't they Sally?' she said, looking at me in the hope I would back her up. I knew that there was no choice; I had to agree with her. I couldn't let her go through this. She was petrified and anyway, she had been brave enough to run with me. I felt that there was no other way but to agree with her and confirm this story, so I agreed, but to my horror the tall tale got worse.

'Yes Dad, we tried to fight them, but they dragged us into the car, didn't they Sally?' she said.

'Yes,' I answered torn between my desire to save us from a beating, and to protect dear Aunty Gwen.

'Are you sure, you little pair of bastards?' said Dad menacingly.

'Yes Dad,' we said in unison looking very positive as the lies rolled up our throats. Well, I mean what else could we say? The lunatic was waiting to savage us.

'What were you doing out of the house anyway?' he asked suddenly realizing this couldn't have possibly happened if we had been in doors where we should have been. He waited with that got ya expression, but we were becoming quick at the outwit me game.

'The babe woke for a drink,' I said. 'We had no milk, so we all went out to nick some bottles off the doorstep - we thought it was best for all of us to go so the babe didn't wake you!' What a crock of crap we had just told him, but he bought it.

'Right, you're the mother now get them down to the cop shop and get the cheeky bastards locked up for kidnapping them,' ordered dad to my mum.

'Right Paddy,' Mum said, grabbing her coat taking me and my sister towards the front door. As we were leaving dad warned, 'Sally, don't change your story, I'm telling you.' So off we went walking down the street in the dark night in our thin cotton dresses.

'Sally, I thought our dad said we were never to tell the police anything about anybody,' my sister whispered. 'He said that was grassing?'

'He must be a lying grass himself then, mustn't he?' I told her.
Once there, Mum made her complaint to the police then took us back home. Dad was sitting on the table waiting for us, 'Right, come here you pair now,' he said. 'You didn't think I was silly enough to believe that load of shite you told me, do you?'

He told my sister he was disgusted with her lack of loyalty, that she had betrayed him and the family and as much as he loved her, he had to teach her never to do that again. He then punched her into the face knocking her to the ground. She did not wake for a few minutes, and he then told Mum to take her to bed while he dealt with Peg-leg.

Turning to me he said sternly, 'Scab, you've double crossed me, haven't you?'

'Yes Dad,' I said staring at the ground, knowing what was to come but unable to run. He punched me in the head which knocked me across the room and thankfully I landed on the settee. I did not seem to be cut, but boy did I see stars.

'Jump to attention Scab,' my father ordered. Like a flash I was on my feet, hands by my side, head up and standing straight like a soldier. Something he had often made me do. 'Now scabby, you're going under the floorboards, with the rats and the spiders tonight,' said Dad. The floorboards were fixed to lift in the corner if the police came for him. It wouldn't take him two seconds to get down there. He'd often threatened to put me down there and I hated the thought of it.

My nightmare was about to become a reality as he pulled up the floorboards ready to put me down. This was a three-to-four-foot drop where he hid when hiding from the police and social workers, NSPCC, and social security officers. I shook as he shoved me down into the pitch-black pit and put the floorboards back. For a few minutes I was in total darkness, then I could see small flickers of light as it came through the chinks in the floorboards. It seemed deep to my tiny frame and was so creepy with a sooty, dusty, hard earth floor. I could see cobwebs hanging from the beams as a dank and dusty smell hit me. I stood stiff and frozen with fear as sweat dripped from my forehead as the horrid sickening feeling entered my gut again. Close to hysteria I moved my eyes around the hole, waiting for the spiders to crawl onto my skin and the rats to bite my ankles.

I heard my father whispering down through the floorboards to me in a spooky bogeyman voice, 'Have the spiders and rats bit you yet Scab? They're coming; they're c-o-m-i-n-g!' feeding my fears. I don't know how long I stayed in that hole, but it seemed like hours. I was trembling and freezing cold when he finally got me out.

'Sit on the settee Scab,' he said. I knew by his voice that there was more to come. I sat for a minute, panic threatening to break out at any minute. 'Get over here Scab, now,' he ordered. I got up and walked over very slowly. My nerves must have been in a desperate state, because as I walked over, I wet myself.

Yes, I took a good beating this night and naturally I couldn't attend school for weeks. It seems I was in Dublin with my grandmother again. I visited her a lot when I carried serious proof of abuse on my body. My Irish trip consisted of me being hid in an empty bedroom, with an old metal bed by the walls and a filthy half curtain across the bottom of the uncleaned broken glass windows. The shabby wallpaper which was ripped all over complemented the manky hovel. I had seen nicer looking toilets in my times and visited less smelling pig sties.

The grubby black marks and hanging wallpaper was a toy to me. I often tore it off to make a pleasant game of shop. I had half a broken pencil and tore bits of paper off and pleasantly played away making shopping lists and speaking to customers, trying to forget the endless horrific circumstances about me and amusing myself so not to die of hours of boredom.

It was difficult to remember my age when all these true events happened in my life. They just did, and so by the time I was about nine, I was a nervous wreck and Dad got even heavier on the drink and continued his abusive behaviours.

The years of abuse had left my mother a broken woman. She was full of fear and so afraid of him by now that she made no attempt to protect me. By today's standards I guess this would be called battered wife syndrome. She stood there, terrified, saying nothing, almost sensitized to it all, while Father became far more bizarre and psychotic. I was more out of school than in it, and the NSPCC were calling regularly.

I continued to run away from home, yet I was always sent back. The NSPCC asked me once why I kept running away. I continued to deny the explanation and proof I had given or shown the police because after all, whatever I said, (and the facts I had marks to prove some of it), I was always sent back because Mother always denied what I said. She gave a reason for my marks of abuse and protected my father.

As far as I was concerned the NSPCC and Social Services were a complete waste of time. I felt trapped in it all with no light at the end of the tunnel. In spite of the facts all these civil servants had their suspicions, and all their red tape processes. Yet the truth is that none of this helped me and as Father became sicker his evilness became even greater. The police officers were on to it and wanted to act but couldn't remove me until Social Services got their fingers out. Apparently, they were being hindered by (get this) lack of proof and red tape. I was still living in this, regardless to my courageous attempts to get out, so slowly but surely, I began to lose any hope of being rescued by those that were in a position to do so. I eventually lost my trust in all people of authority.

Mum and Dad started to go out every night and at times stayed out all night. Dad would tie the door key around my neck as they left and I would have to clean the house again, bath the kids in the old-fashioned washing boiler, and after settling them down to bed, I would wait nervously for Dad to return. It never went quite as smoothly as that but that was the general routine that I attempted. At about half past ten I began to get very restless as terrible butterflies gripped my tummy, so, by the time I heard his steel cap shoes coming down the yard, I was shivering in my boots. I had learned to operate with fear for so long now that I didn't know how to function without it.

One night I was lying on the settee with the big door key tied around my neck and I dozed off. Suddenly, I heard someone staggering down the yard. I recognised the drunken voice of my mother singing. Oh-my-gosh! I shit myself, and rightly so too, for this night I was beaten senseless again. For what I do not know, but I think it was simply because I was me. I knew for certain I was an unwanted member of this family and an unwelcome person in this place.

CHAPTER 15

I hated Dad with a vengeance by now and loathed the ground he walked on. As polite as I was to his face, he knew my true feelings. He wasn't daft. I had been in the house a few years and as each day passed, I still could not understand the way of life of these people. To me, this house and these people were filth and poverty at its worst. My siblings hadn't got a chance being raised in such an environment. The children's nails, necks, knees, and feet were often filthy, yet even though I was dressed tattily and poorly, I made sure to keep my skin as spotless as possible.

It seemed that my mother knew when the NSPCC Officer was due and would get stuck into spring cleaning the pit and scrubbing the children before she arrived. If she did happen to call while the house was in a mess, or Mum had black eyes or bruises from a beating, she would take us into the kitchen making us all stay quiet until she went. Now and again, she caught her though.

You see the front door was in the front room and there was no-way to quieten and remove my siblings now for they had been heard and in-fact the NSPCC officer was peering through the letter box telling my little brother to get Mummy. I loved it when they got outwitted like this but just wished they would put as much energy into getting me out as they were obviously building their case.

'Quick Paddy it's that one from the cruelty to children place,' she whispered urgently knowing the Officer was chatting to my little brother through the letter box and wasn't moving. To Mum's horror the little one was replying to her and shouting to Mum, 'Mums coming - she's just hiding daddy.'

I ran over and picked him up saying, 'No she's not you silly billy your always saying daft things.' Deep down I thought it was so funny. I could never understand how so much deceit seemed to dance past all these professionals, but I guess times were very different back then. I am sure they were on to something - their regular appearances at our home and school proved this, but what was holding them up from acting upon our situation?

They tried to get me alone and question me and would often come the following day, after I had run away. The police would read my accusations to them, and you'll never guess what they did. They came to my house and called Mum to account on all I had told the police placing me in even more danger. For as long as I remember after that my mother accused me of swearing my father's life away to the police.

Mother always had an excuse because I always retracted what I said so I always ended up staying and suffering the consequences of my decisions to run and tell. I often wondered why they never came to the police station to interview me where I felt safe and would have told all. But no such luck, the Social Worker who took over from the NSPCC I think, would always ask me the same questions and I always gave the same answers. She asked if I was happy at home, whereby I would answer, 'Yes.' Then she would ask, 'Is there anything I would like to talk to her about?' To which I would reply, 'No.'

She often asked were things okay with my mother and supposedly elusive Father. To which I would answer, 'Mothers fine and my father does not live with us.' I had been trained well and become a pretty good liar over the past few years. And I couldn't risk anything else I dared to say reaching my parents ears. Unintentionally the very people that had been sent to protect me, were putting my life in greater risk with their approach in dealing with our case. So, I knew I had no choice but to lie yet deep down I yearned to tell the truth and beg her to get me out of there put me into care. Yet that was too much of a massive risk for me, for I knew that whatever I said would be brought to the attention of my mother and that would have been far too dangerous. That's why I never opened my mouth to them - for when I did it always went wrong.

As time went by the only feeling of warmth, love and just a little happiness I felt was the occasional smile from my brothers and sisters or some rude joke they shared with me. I

I'm not sure how old I was when my mother announced she was pregnant again. Oh, she was thrilled, likewise my father, but I wasn't because I knew it was only more responsibility for me.

I found very little time to play out with my brothers and sisters as it was. Scrubbing and caring for everyone took its toll and another child for me to Mother and look after was unthinkable. Many a time as I worked away at my daily never-ending chores, I would hear the loud laughter of my siblings as they played merrily with their friends outside. As I cleaned the bedroom, I often gazed out at them for a moment and watched them as they jumped about at the top of the yard and chased each other about.

They made themselves out of old wood, bricks and rope, a do-it-yourself park. It was very dangerous really. Plus, everybody had to step over lots of bricks to get into the fun but once they did that, there was a seesaw made from a big plank and a thick rope hanging from the scaffolds which was great to swing across to the other condemned house. But had someone fallen, they would have been cut to pieces or surely killed.

There was another thick rope tied across each condemned house, so the children could go across by their hands pretending to cross a dangerous river and of course there was the scaffold where they pretended to be in the circus and do acrobatics on. There were the times that I did manage to get out to play with my family. I got lost in the fantasy of it all forgetting my troubles for a short while having the time of my life with them all, even though nine times out of ten I was forced to babysit my baby brother whilst out there.

Once out of the house I would take the little one up to where my family played and sit watching them, loving the excitement. They were daring little buggers, so I always kept a sharp eye on them all and the littlest one got over excited and always went nuts to get involved. Not to say, he was a strong boy, so it got quite hard work at times trying to restrain him. If he had run off and got hurt, it would have been woe-be-tide me. Sometimes my younger sister gave me a break and held on to him for a while so I could have a quick go on everything, and it was great. If there was to be an accident it was always then, and boy did that mean trouble for me.

By now Dad drank day and night. He'd go to the boozers about 12pm and return after they closed at 3pm. So, depending on the mood I would get it at three as well as 11pm. Sometimes he just mentally terrorized me then went off to bed. Other times, he went off to bed ordering us to give him a wake-up call about six pm so he could get ready and go out again.

He seemed to be the best dressed person in the house. Always spotless with well pressed trousers which he did himself with wet brown paper to make the creases stick. His T-shirts were immaculate or new. He always suited light colours such as white or lemon. He was stocky but had a muscley body that looked great in what he wore. Depending on the weather he wore a jacket or suit, which got pawned with his shoes most Mondays until Mum's Social Security pay day. His shoes were black leather lace ups, the fashion of the time and I don't think I ever saw them less than beautifully polished.

At times, after I had received a good beating and the marks had faded a little, Mum would feel a little sorry for me and tell me I could go out to play with my brothers and sisters for a while, as long as I made sure to get back in the house before Dad came home. At these times when I went out I had so much on my mind; I would go to our self-made park where my siblings screamed with excitement and laughed with joy, but I just sat watching them sadly as I felt far too nervous to play.

By the time it came to this time of my life I was endlessly trembling, jumping out of my skin at any sound and having nightmares when I eventually slept. Most of the time I found it hard to sleep, but once I slept, I found it hard to wake. I was always tired and lacked energy, but I had to find what I needed to work and get through each day. Day to day I had to struggle with griping tummy pains and heart palpations. I didn't know what was happening to me, but I knew there was something awfully wrong. But it was no good requesting a doctor in this place if your name happened to be Sally. I never needed to attention seek for as you can see, I was always getting attention. I never complained - I never dared. It seemed the more obedient I was the worse I was treated.

Anyway, mother being pregnant again I guess I had to find more strength for the forth coming little one. One night as I made tea for my parents after they returned from the pub, Mum suddenly went into labour. My Father rushed for the midwife to my surprise, while I tried to support and comfort my mother. I gently helped her into the bed that had been brought down into the front room ready for this occasion. The sheets and house were spotless ready for this. I'd helped Mum to get it and keep it so. After she was settled, I started boiling pots of water for the midwife. After returning with her my dad came into the kitchen and sat talking to me.

It was on these very rare times that I saw an utterly different side to him, maybe even a side I could have come to like, possibly even love.

'You're a good kid Sal – we've got a long night ahead,' he said as I kept boiling pots of water and cleaning up. The midwife opened the kitchen door telling Dad that Mum's waters had broken, but she still had a long way to go. We had been in the kitchen for hours listening to Mums screams or loud moans even growling at times. Now and again the midwife come in for something which I had to take into her. She said I was a fine little nurse and was doing an amazing job. At other times I sat on the stairs by Dad, and he would chat to me and nicely as though he was truly grateful for my company and helpfulness. Talk about Jackal and Hyde. In-spite of the noise in the living room, the other kids remained upstairs and never woke once through-out the night.

'What do you think Mum will have Sal?'

'A boy Dad,' I said confused by how nice he was being to me.

'Well, I hope so kid, we don't want another little split-arse hay?' said Dad in a cheery tone that I wasn't used to. As the hours passed away, I made endless cups of tea. Towards the end of the night, we could hear Mum breathing fast and moaning loudly. I dozed off for a while on the stairs and woke at about ten to six in the morning.

'Do you want tea Dad?' I asked yawning.

'Okay Sal,' he replied.

We could hear things clearly from the living room now, and by the sounds of things Mum was giving birth to the baby. As I poured the tea, we kept looking at the door as the midwife shouted continuously, 'Push, come on, again, Push!'

Our tea break was interrupted by the first screams of the baby and the midwife rushed in and told Dad he had a son. In the middle of what she was saying Mum screamed again and the midwife went back to her rapidly. The door was slightly ajar, so Dad and I tried peeping at the newcomer when suddenly we overheard the midwife, 'Good gracious Mrs Murphy we have another baby coming!'

'Oh no tell me you're joking nurse,' groaned my Mum.

'No, I'm not Mrs Murphy you're having twins my dear,' replied the midwife, beginning to laugh. 'Now come on its time to push again! That's the girl.

'Push!' she encouraged her a few more times and then it happened - the second boy was born. They were underweight, so my father was asked to go and get an ambulance, 'Mr Murphy, just walk through here, you don't have to look. Call for a doctor at once and two incubators.'

'Right Nurse,' said Dad and off he went. I can never recall him taking orders from a woman before, but he did. The nurse called me in, 'Sally, come and see the babies before they go to bed you've been a fantastic help. Mrs Murphy you have a beautiful daughter here - what a great help she must be to you. Now come peep at your baby brothers Sally before they go you truly deserve to my dear!'

I stood up to go when I heard my Mum say, 'No, call her other sister to see them.'

'Mrs, Murphy, Sally has been here all night helping us,' said the confused midwife. 'Shouldn't she be the first one who gets to see the babies before they go?'

'No Nurse,' persisted my Mum. 'Sally won't mind. Call her other sister please.' So, she did, and my sister came down to see the twins. I could see by the nurse's face that she was not comfortable with that decision at all, and she gave me a caring knowing smile. Truth was, I did mind, I minded very much and felt really hurt and angry with my mother for that. I went off to bed but for the life of me I could not understand my mother's logic in that last act. To me it was simply another slap in the face and another nail of rejection in my emotional coffin.

CHAPTER 16

One day after I had returned from school, I sat on the settee looking at my Father who seemed to be in a drunken sleep and silently prayed that he might die in his slumber. Mum busied herself in the kitchen as Dad began to wake. Suddenly he looked at me and said, 'What you looking at Scab?'

'Nothing Dad,' I said looking at the floor.
'What's that smell?' he said turning his face away. 'For f*** sake that's disgusting! Smells like rotten flesh, it's bad - what the hell is it?' I began to feel a little uneasy knowing only too well the smell was coming from my leg.

'I wonder has an animal got into the house and died. I have smelt this before in the army, its dead flesh I am telling you women!'
Father began hunting out the source of the smell. Suddenly he looked at me and then at my leg, 'Mother in here quick,' he beckoned. 'The smell's coming from her leg. Be-jez-us, that stinks rotten,' he said backing away from me shooting Mum a concerned look. 'This could be real trouble,' he told her, staring at my leg the worry on his face plain to see. He asked me to let him take a look.

'I would dad, but I can't get my sock off,' I replied. With that my father began to try and remove my sock, but seeing it was hurting me more than I cared to say, he stopped trying to pull it off and told my mother to fetch some water from the kitchen so he could bathe it off, 'Why didn't you tell us your leg was this bad Sally?' he asked.

'I was scared to Dad,' I replied simply. He ordered Mum to get some more fresh warm water and when she returned Dad began to bathe my leg very gently until finally, he got the sock off. Looking at my leg I could see my father was horrified, and rightly so too. My leg had two holes on the side which seemed to be eating through my flesh. One was deep and festered with blood-stained green and yellow pus flowing from it. The smell was indescribable. The other hole was much smaller but otherwise the same as the larger hole. They were both very raw with red flesh swelling around the outside of the wound and around that was a ring of really white flesh.

Father, still quite shaken, pulled Mum aside and then went out saying he was off to get an ambulance and not to worry, he would not be long. Meanwhile Mum began to wash my feet and body as she talked to me in a kind way. This was totally out of character for her and although I accepted it at the time and responded to her kindness, it made me feel very uncomfortable. I could read her like a book and see that it was all false but so starved of affection was I that I'd rather play along than accept the truth.

It wasn't long before the ambulance arrived, and my mother came along with me to the children's hospital. When we arrived at the hospital, two doctors came in and looked at my leg. One then took my mother outside. They wanted to keep me in hospital, but Mum wouldn't have that and so after many tests and covering the wound with a burn gauze and other stuff, they let me go home for the night, telling my mother before we left that it was very important that I returned to the hospital the next day as Doctor Allen would surely wish to see me. We were returned home by ambulance and my mother settled me comfortably on the settee before going down to the pub to meet my father.

That night my father returned home with my mother, and they were both quite drunk. Dad began to get a little nasty with me for bringing shame on the family. My Mother was not having this tonight and jumped up in front of him shouting, 'Leave it out Allen I've got to face the f***ing authorities not you! You're not touching her tonight – or as true as God, you will take her tomorrow. If you don't, they will come here, and I'll tell them everything. I swear to God I will.'

'She needs a good belting for this,' he said. 'We could be in a load of trouble through it,' he said lifting his hand ready to aim. But Mum grabbed his arm before he could make contact. 'Don't you dare Paddy Murphy. If this kid's got one mark on her when I take her back to the hospital tomorrow, I'll tell them straight you did it so help me God I will.'

'You know you wouldn't do that,' he said but the look on his face showed that he wasn't sure.

At the hospital they wanted to know why my leg was allowed to get into such a condition and how my mother did not notice it. It seems they told her she should have taken me to the Doctors long before now.

Mum began to say to my father, 'They think Sally's had a bang on the leg and ripped which got infected. I told them that I had a big family, and she was probably kicked messing about with them. They said she's got ulcers which have gone bad ways, and they can't understand how her leg's been left unnoticed for so long.'

'F*** them,' said Dad.

'Let's see how clever you are in the morning without your bottle Paddy. Do you even realise what I'm trying to tell you?' said Mum.

'Yes, sure I do, you silly bitch,' he replied.

'Well, listen for once,' she said. 'Our Sally might have gangrene and if so, she could lose her leg.' Leaving the revelation hanging in the air, she went into the kitchen sobbing. Suddenly she returned with something in her hand. In horror I realised it was a bread knife. I sat on the settee with my well bandaged leg up looking at my crazed Mother as she waved a bread knife about in our front room.

'You did this to her, you dirty, mad bastard,' she said pointing it at my father. 'You're the one who keeps booting her legs and always battering her -you can't keep your hands off her you dirty animal. It's not right. If our Sally loses that leg Paddy, I swear on my babies' lives, I'll stab you to death. You won't sleep I promise you because I really will kill you.'

I didn't doubt for a moment that she meant it. She became very stressed or had an over whelming fit of guilt and fell to her knees dropping the knife and pulling at her own hair in a mad rage as she poured out an endless volley of anger at my father.

As I looked at my poor Mother, I was filled with an overwhelming pity. I knew she had never been a good Mother, but also realised that fate had been cruel to Mother as much as me, and it was not entirely her fault things were the way they were. My eyes drifted to my father who sat in a daze, his face white and drawn. He didn't seem drunk anymore. The shock of what my mother was saying must have sobered him up. Somehow, I did not feel scared anymore. I knew I wasn't going to be beaten this night. I looked around at these poor pathetic people and a feeling of superior strength came over me. Yes, I might have been weaker physically, but I felt I was the strongest mentally.

At that moment the words of a teacher came to me - 'Sarah is a born leader with the courage of a lion.' I felt that was true. It was right. My Father might go around like the roaring lion, but my inner strength could match him any day. For me to hear that I might have my leg cut off was difficult to take in. *If Dr Allen has to chop my leg off it must be very poorly*. I thought. *But I don't mind because I know Dr Allen will give me a lovely new leg, so it won't be ugly like this one anymore.*

Suddenly a tremendous and joyous thought came to mind, *I'll be with my Sister Brendon and Aunty Gwen again*. I saw this as the only chance to be with the people I loved so dearly, and I began to get excited. In my mind I would have sacrificed more than my leg to be back with them. All my carefully concealed memories came to the forefront of my mind. I pictured my Aunty Gwen's face and began to think of how much I loved her. This woman - my mother - I loved her too, but I could never love her in the way that I loved my Aunty Gwen. I hated this filthy house, but I dearly loved these children. They may have been dirty, scruffy, and noisy, but they were funny, loveable and all I had. My Father, well, I suppose I tolerated him, but I hated the way he continued to treat me.

My Mother continued to throw verbal abuse his way as she went through varying stages of hysteria and self-pity. My Father gazed at her for a moment as a look of compassion crossed his face. He got up, walked over to her, and gently lifted her into his arms and carried her up to bed. Shortly afterwards he went back downstairs. I winced as he sat down beside me, 'Sally, do you hate me?'

'No Dad,' I replied bracing myself for the obligatory beating that normally followed this question. But this time was different, 'You need to forgive me for what I do to you at times, Sally,' he went on to say with a look on his face that I wasn't used to. He almost looked normal. 'I don't really want to hurt you kid. I love you Sally, but at times I can't help what I do and believe me kid, I suffer for it,' he continued. 'It cripples me when I see what I've done to you when I'm sober. It's the drink Sally; your dad's sick so please try not to hate me too much.' With that last plea he turned and looked me fully in the face.

'I know that Dad, it's okay,' I mumbled, just glad that the usual beating didn't seem on the cards.

'Remember Sally, deep at heart your dad loves you very much and take note of what I'm saying to you now,' he said, still looking at me intensely. 'If anything should ever happen to your old Dad, I love the lot of you.' At times like this it was like he was talking about another person.

'I will Dad, I promise,' I said. 'But what do you mean if anything should happen to you? I don't understand what you are saying?'

'Well, you know your old Dad's always fighting,' he said. 'Some day somebody will get really mad with me and come looking for your dad to put him away for ever. Do you understand Sally?'

'Yes, I do, Dad,' I replied knowing full well what he meant and not liking the thought of what he was saying to me. Even though I had wished it upon him so many times the actual thought of him dead filled me with sadness. This conversation puzzled me somewhat. Usually, I took little heed of his words when he'd been drinking. He was always saying that someone would kill him one day. But this particular conversation stuck out in my mind. I found myself thinking about it for ages after.

He then knelt in front of me and began to sing a song I had heard him sing many times before, only this time it seemed to have a strong meaning, 'When you walk through a storm, hold your head up high, and don't be afraid of the dark. At the end of the storm there's a golden sky, and the sweet silver song of a lark. Walk on through the wind, walk on through the rain, though your dreams be tossed and blown. Walk on, walk on, with hope in your heart and you'll never walk alone, you'll never walk alone again.'

He sang it beautifully as tears rolled from his eyes. Despite everything he'd done to me I was overcome with warmth and pity for him. It was at this point that I fully realised that my father was a very sick man who desperately wanted somebody's help because he wasn't strong enough to seek it himself. We chatted once more for a little while, and then he very gently carried me up the stairs to bed, trying very hard not to bang or hurt my leg as he did so.

CHAPTER 17

Arriving at the Birmingham children's hospital the next morning, I was taken straight from registration to see Dr Allen who had deep concerns regarding my welfare and wanted to know how my leg got into such a state un-noticed. My Mother became very uncomfortable for it was so obvious by Doctor Allen's questions and expressions, that he did not believe a single word she was saying. He was extremely abrupt with her at times and seemed somewhat disgusted by her feeble answers. I guess that could have been perceived as unprofessional, but truth be known, he was a professional man to the core, that does not mean he was heartless.

This specialist knew my story; he had been my orthopaedic surgeon since I was a baby. We had many a childish battle in years gone by, as he tried to give me an examination of the feet, hips, and legs whilst in St Gerald's hospital. He always had a party trick up his sleeve and would pull a bag of sweets out of his pocket just for me and then I hushed up and gave in willingly. I am so glad today that I never continued that behaviour through life, showing men my legs for gifts.

Doctor Allen, who in-fact was so highly qualified he was actually called Mr Allen, then told Mother that he wanted me in hospital at once, but she would not agree to it. He tried repeatedly to persuade her to change her mind - to no avail. She simply wouldn't have it, but what the hospital staff did not realize was that it was more than her life was worth to go against my father. To agree to allow me to go into hospital where there was a good chance that I might spill the beans on Dad was her worst fear. Oh, she wanted him to stop him, and to stop hurting me, she just didn't know how to safely do that. Let's face it, she wasn't the most intelligent person, and all the professional jargon was way beyond her understanding most of the time. She didn't trust the authorities because my father didn't trust them. Remember unknown to anyone, she was under strict orders from my father who incidentally was waiting over the road in a shop doorway, because he didn't seem to have the balls to come over and face the music himself.

I was kept in the cubical with a nurse, while Mum was asked to wait and talk to Dr Allen. He told her that he felt very strongly that I had to be hospitalized immediately; he said he couldn't understand her strong stand against this. He wanted to know her issue with it. He explained that I needed immediate treatment to deal with the infection which was eating into my flesh and spreading. He asked her did she realize how serious this matter was and tried to impress upon her the enormity of it. I may have been in a cubical in Mr Allen's office, but I wasn't deaf and could hear it all.

He went on to explain to her that his concerns for my health were so strong that he felt he needed to call the Social Services and intended to do just that. Mother quietly protested, and his final word to her on this matter was, 'In refusing to acknowledge the gravity of Sarah's situation, you give me little choice Mrs Murphy!'

'Wait a minute Doctor please; I need a few minutes to think about it. Can I take a breath of fresh air please?' He agreed to wait a few minutes, and I knew Mum had run over the road to Dad, cowering in the doorway as he left Mum to face the aftermath of my neglected infected leg. She hurried back almost breathless as she entered Mr Allen's office and trying to catch her breath, she told him to admit me into hospital.

I was unsure to why the Doctor was so determined to have his way that day. Was I really so sick that I needed urgent hospital assistance, or was there a slight possibility, that this was a combined opportunity for the authorities to get me out of my position in life for a while?

I am unsure if a Social Worker ever came, I was just ecstatic knowing that I was out of there for a while, away from all the violence and horror. I can't remember being this excited in years. I was free for a while. No more beatings and pain. It was unbelievable, but I couldn't let my mother see my joy to it all for she might change her mind and take me home. I wasn't about to take that risk. So, I pretended I was sad about being taken away from home. Mother came up and hugged me. Before she left, she put something in my hands, 'Here Sally, it's not much, but you can read a bit, can't you? It's all I have.'

'Thanks Mum,' I said unsure how to respond to this unexpected gift.

I was utterly touched by her actions, and very moved when I saw what she had given me. It was a small, red, shabby, well used old Bible. She might have picked it up at some second-hand shop; but nevertheless, her act of kindness deeply impressed me. My-gosh, I was completely taken aback by this. I had never seen this caring, sensitive side to my mother, not towards me anyway. What a lovely thing to do. More so, considering this took a lot of courage and was a very risky act, for if my father found out it would have seen as going against his wishes, and encouraging me to keep believing in those biblical writings which in his opinion was nothing but pure bullshit.

My response seemed to please Mum and she said, 'Good, read it if you can Sal, but hide it if your dad comes to see you - you know what he's like about these things.'

'Yes Mum, thank you,' I said throwing my arms around her neck for a second or two. Maybe she did love me after all; she just probably didn't know how to show it.

I realize today, it wasn't her fault, it was just the way she was, but it was obvious she struggled with displays of affection towards me, for she was fine with her other children.

I was happy but stunned at this gift. For one I was still quite young even though I had to grow up fast. I always wanted one of those pictured children's Bibles, but nevertheless I saw this present as the best she could do, and in-fact a very thoughtful gift and I loved her for it.

So often I have wondered why she had that Bible for she couldn't read or write. She knew I could read enough to get by, but I wasn't that great, certainly not enough for the complication of such theological writings. At my age a children's Bible was pictured and simplified for my understanding and of cause in Aunty Gwen's Church, we weren't ministered to by Pastors, instead we attended the Sunday school section of the church.

At St Gerald's we all attended mass and although I knew about Jesus and Hail Mary and even Bible stories, I hadn't a clue in those times what the Priest was talking about. Thinking about it all now, the masses were so beautiful, and all in Latin. The songs of praise from Nuns as they worshiped the mighty God were breath taking, and at times the songs and chanting hymns of the Monks we're amazing. Even children would sit in awe as if it quietened their spirits for a time.

I was sent to an open-air hospital in Malvern which is a gorgeous part of the West Midlands and I stayed there for three months. The respite was amazing. The events I had suffered seemed so far away. I never had a visitor, but I didn't care. At least I was free from the hell I had experienced, for a little while anyway and this suited me down to the ground. This was such an opportunity to tell everyone what had been going on in my life but due to the lack of action on the part of the professional organizations in my case, I felt it too risky to open my mouth again. No-one was telling me I wouldn't be returning. Yes, as crazy as this decision was, it seemed safer for me to stay silent.

I remember looking in my locker one day at hospital and Mum's little red Bible fell out. I looked at it as it fell open on one page. I tried to read it in my girlish fashion, but it didn't make sense. So, I held it on that page until the nurse came to say hi to me and asked her to read what the Bible was saying, because people had told me the Bible is God's word. I felt as if this little red book had God's word in it meaning he is speaking directly to us, and I wanted to know what He was saying to me this day. She read 2 Corinthians 6:14, 'Do not be yoked together with unbelievers.' *Wow*! I thought. *That's my dad - he doesn't believe in Jesus.* I asked the nurse for a few more explanations for I was always inquisitive child who loved to learn.

As I got older, I felt blessed with a gift of bringing creative thoughts to life. I was in my element discovering the vastness of my imagination. I wasn't afraid to be different and give anything that seemed a good idea a go, even though others often felt it was pie in the sky through-out my life.

I spent a wonderful three months in that hospital but sadly the day was rapidly arriving that I would have to return home, and I began to dread it. I was so well looked after and fussed over in here which was such a huge contrast from what I'd left behind. I was treated as a child and allowed to be the true child I really was. The troubling thoughts of having to leave all this normality to return to that dysfunctional reality horrified me.

The convalescence hospital was such a wonderful place set in glorious ground, and we patients had full access to it all. The building was like huge mansion which was turned into hospital wards inside. It was spotlessly clean and peaceful (apart from sick patients moaning or calling nurse of a night) and it was so lovely to have my own clean bed again -with a pillow, sheets, and clean warm blankets which. incidentally were changed twice a day.

My skin had also become a big concern for the staff on my arrival and it was obvious to most of the staff and hospital doctors that I was a seriously neglected child. I had to be creamed three times a day and my arms and legs were bandaged like a mummy. I was also grossly underweight, and my hair was extremely thin. I needed vitamins as well as other treatments, like little blue tablets to stop the eczema itching and medicines for the infection in my leg, and that had to be redressed twice a day too. I learned how to relax here, and I found a little happiness in life again.

Soon the dreaded day came when it was time to return to my home. This thought was not pleasing to me at all. Apart from the filth which would surely spark my eczema off, I knew that if my mother didn't apply my cream twice a day and make sure I took my medicine, my skin problem was sure to flare up again. Never in a million years would she keep this up because as far as my parents were concerned, I was big enough and ugly enough to do it myself. I could only hope the stiff talking to she had received from Mr Allen may have been a wakeup call for her, and out of sheer embarrassment not to have to face that situation again, she might make sure it was done. Although deep down I was sure that after a few days my treatment would be pushed aside, and I would be reeled in and rapidly brought back to my father's way of thinking.

CHAPTER 18

I returned home and it was wonderful to see my fabulous little siblings who we're overjoyed to see me again. Mum was herself and Dad left me alone for a short while, giving me time to settle back into my old way of living, which I now knew only too well. My mother had also been told how important it was for me to attend my orthopaedic outpatients' appointments and the doctor's surgery, so that my skin complaint could be monitored and kept under control.

But it was only a matter of weeks before my parents had me back into the old routine of general dogsbody, Mum's emotional battering post and Dad's living punch bag. I hated coming back to this. There was no appreciation at all from these people to the fact that I had kept my mouth shut and most likely certainly kept my father out of prison. As time went by and I was compliant to their orders, I still refused to accept this way of life. I couldn't understand for the life of me the craziness in the way these people thought and behaved.

By now I had seven siblings, imagine that. In a two-bedroom, old fashioned house lived eight children and two parents - ten of us, with no hot water, no bathroom, and no inside toilet. Can you begin to understand the suffocating effects of having to live in that place?

What I always found interesting was that my mother continued to have babies and live off the state and each time a new baby came along, she got more family allowances, and she had a rise in her social security payments. Having said that my father was not living with us and didn't know where he was, they must have thought she was a right old Trollope.

Mum was conning the dole because my father was a bum who was too lazy to work and support his wife and children. You know, it may not have been acceptable, but it was certainly understandable why Mother was doing this. In a sense she had no choice, for even though my father did live with her, I only ever remember him working for a very short while once.

He was pouncing off Mum, sadly taking what little she had. He brought no money into our house at all but took a huge chunk of the income out of it. Our weekly allowance awarded by the state was to be spent on food, rent and bills and for herself and her children, but no such luck. They spent like there was no tomorrow in the pub on booze, day and night. I mean, had he been living with us doing a bit of cash in hand - work on the side - each week, and handing money over to help provide for his kids, many might understand that. He could at least have paid for his own alcohol, but he was doing none of this so really Mum was only guilty of having him live there, but it was so sad to see the amount of power my father had over my mother's life.

She went to any lengths for him and would have done anything to keep him around. This man was so low he could have crawled under a snake's belly with a top hat on. I couldn't say my father's drinking got any worse, because by now it was at its worst - for us to have to tolerate and live with anyway. He was a monster when he took a drink. From dawn to dusk his moods rapidly changed and with that our moods had to comply. We were always treading on eggshells around him, but after he took a drink, we were petrified. He was the meanest spirited person I had ever met in life and has much as I disliked him, I began to realize he was a very sick person. That's what mum said anyway.

She would say to me at times, 'Don't hate your Da Sally, it's the drink it makes him sick. He goes mad on the stuff, and I can't get him to stop.'

I heard what she was saying and even understood, but I had to smile, for was this not the kettle calling the pot black. I felt like screaming at her, 'Never mind him, why don't you stop and help me out here cleaning your home and raising your kids?'

My gosh, this was a clear case of chronic alcoholism within a family and the desperate devastation and sheer madness we children had to try and understand and cope with was too much. I didn't know whether I was coming or going, I didn't know whether to laugh or to cry. I was afraid every day, never knowing what to expect. My once bubbly personality had gone and I'd become silent, sullen, and withdrawn. I lived in a constant state of fear, which by the end of the day had turned to terror. Even in my dreams I was tormented.

Nobody really understood the disease of alcoholism back then, so to me he was simply a vile person when he had a drink and that's exactly what I thought he was - a vile, evil person. It was to take many years before we came to realize the true facts of the matter and the root of all our problems. I found my father trying to kill himself a few times, and there were many times I wished he had succeeded.

One night in particular, I remember it happening on his return from the pub, he had found yet another reason to make my life a misery. He called me over to his chair stinking drunk and said, 'The biggest mistake of your life was the time you pulled my head out of the gas oven Sally, what a silly little Bastard you are!'

In the next breath he taunted me and accused me of putting his head in it. I felt like screaming at him, 'You fat evil basket-case - how could I drag your pissed up heavy body to the stove and put your massive sick big head in the oven? Can't you see it does not make sense! I am a kid and even I can see that.'

But I never had the guts to say what I thought loudly, no, I had more sense than that. I had what I call anger thoughts and silent outbursts to try and deal with my endless frustrations.

He had gone beyond understanding now and all I knew was that I feared him more than anything I had ever known. It didn't matter if he was drunk or sober; I jumped when he looked at me and trembled even if he touched me harmlessly. I lived on nervous energy, and it was getting to the stage whereby I got very little sleep. I'd lie shaking in case I should be woken up with a punch in the face or just dragged out of the bed by my hair, which had happened so often before. I was afraid to sleep, yet afraid to stay awake.

In the day I crept about the house like a terrified dog and at night I lay for hours shaking and crying silently until my body took over and I would drift into a sort of catnap. But at the slightest movement I found myself jumping into a sitting position in the bed, where I sat trembling for hours. I was finding it difficult to cope but it was far too dangerous not to, so I had to try and find a way to continue.

I was under tremendous stress, tired, hungry, and over worked - undoubtedly suffering from exhaustion and demonstrating some very worrying signs. I couldn't always remember the days of the week. I didn't even know the month I was living in at times. I rarely attended school, and for me there simply seemed no light at the end of this tunnel and no escape route to get me out. I felt doomed and wondered could I even take any-more. So, it was in the early years of my childhood that I first began to flirt with the idea of suicide.

It was nearing my birthday and even though I wasn't too sure of anything anymore, I had a feeling it was near. As a rule, I didn't get a slapping at Christmas, Easter or on my birthday. Yet Father's unpredictable conduct now may suddenly put a change to that. I thought of other children getting all excited and longing for their parties, birthday cake and presents, but for me I knew that was in days far gone. The most appreciated gift for me could only be to have a break and not take a whopping that day.

Every day I woke up with much to do and most days went to bed black and blue. Every day for two weeks I thought, *it will be okay today; it must be my birthday so I won't get hit and I may get a gift like the other children*. I was sure my birthday must be near now, so this day I went to my Mum and said, 'Mum, it's my birthday in a few days, isn't it?'

'No Sally, your Birthday was two weeks ago!' came the reply.

I couldn't believe it, no little gift no happy birthday greetings, no little cake, and no happy birthday song. I was so sad. I felt about as important as the shit and piss bucket on the landing to this family. Nobody had remembered my birthday and what really concerned me now was the fact that even I didn't remember when my tenth birthday was. *What kid forgets their tenth birthday?* I thought sadly.

Talking about the time I caught Dad trying to kill himself, one night I was woken by what I thought was a smell of gas. I tipped toed downstairs and saw Dad lying on the kitchen floor with a folded coat under his head and his head in the gas oven. I was stunned and didn't know what to do. I stood frozen to the spot on the final stair step staring at his very still body and facing the biggest decision of my young life.

That gas is strong. I should get him out or he will die but if I get him out, he will end up killing me. Let him die Sally, I thought. Then I thought about my brothers and sisters. I couldn't let them die. I had to turn the gas off. *Then open the windows and just leave him there. Why should you help him he only hurts you? If you leave him, he can never beat you and defile you again, let the wicked bastard die he deserves it.*

Boy it was only seconds yet in my mind it seemed like hours. I walked over to Dad turned the gas off and tried to pull his head out. I ran upstairs and got Mum who helped me, and we managed to get him out. Mum called an ambulance and off he was carted; he was fine and returned home the next day.

I recall another time I walked into the toilet and caught him with his leather belt around his neck trying to hang himself from the old-fashioned flush system. The chain was over the head over the toilets in those days. He was never grateful for me finding him – in fact he utterly resented me for it.

These beatings all became a little too much for me and one day I decided I had taken enough. So, early one morning while my father was still in a drunken sleep from the night before, I got dressed and robbing a few shillings from Mum's purse I ran away. I wandered about for ages until in the end I jumped on a bus and ended up God knows where. It snowed as I roamed the dark streets frozen with cold and wishing I had robbed Mum's coat. I felt like the little matchstick girl in the fairy story roaming the cold streets - freezing. I was determined never to return to that house again.

Eventually the police found me under a canvas sleeping in somebody's green house. They had heard some pottering about in their garden and green house so had called the police. As always, the police sent me home and informed the Social Workers the following morning, then we had our usual visit from them.

When the coast was clear a few days later, as always, the moment I dreaded arrived, and in came Daddy dearest with Mum. Then it was time for me to face the consequences of my disloyalty and betrayal. Betrayal they called it, well I never, and there was me thinking I was simply trying to survive.

Father did something so horrific to me this night. He called me down the stairs and trembling I slowly walked towards him as he always demanded. We were standing at the gas cooker, and he said, 'Tonight you die Scab.' I looked at his heartless face and I knew that I was in serious trouble. I could hear my heart pounding as I looked around at the door to see if I could get out, but the door was bolted from the top and I had no chance.

I thought that if I got out and ran screaming, even if he caught me, someone was sure to hear and call the police. *This time they would surely catch him.* It seemed it was better to die on my feet trying, than on my knees begging. Alas there seemed no choice, for Father's way it was going to be.

'Turn the gas on Sally,' he demanded.

I looked at him and said, 'Oh no Daddy please!'

'Turn the f****** gas on scab then kneel down and put your head in it now, before I whip you and then make you do it. Save yourself some pain and do it now!'

My hand trembled as I turned the gas on, knelt and put my head in it. When he felt like I'd had enough, he turned the gas off and got me out. He seemed to enjoy this barbaric act of torture and did it to me many more times over the next eight months. I never knew each time I knelt and put my head in that oven if I would stand up again and walk away from it alive.

CHAPTER 19

You might think things couldn't get worse for me but sadly they did. Something happened in my life at this point which changed my way of thinking for ever. If there had ever been a happy, go lucky, sweet, adorable, loving little Sarah in me, she was about to be overpowered by a bitter, angry, hateful, resentful little Sally.

This memory began early one Sunday morning. It could have only been five am. My parents had been out drinking most of the night and had only returned from the night club a few hours previously. Mother was unconscious in drunken sleep upstairs, and I don't think she could have woken if the house had fallen down. All my siblings including myself were fast asleep in bed, when suddenly the bedroom door opened to where my sister and I slept.

It didn't take much to wake me, so I sat up sharply and heard my father's voice whispering, 'Get up Sally and follow me downstairs - be quiet and don't wake your sister.' I jumped up quickly as quietly as I could and slowly made my way down the stairs, trembling and anxiously wondering what is this all about.

Well, he's not shouting or hurting me, I thought as he told me to sit in front of him on the chair. Maybe I had to clean the house or do something for him. Oh my, do something for him was right.

Everything was silent as Dad continued to stare at me. I looked around the room and quickly at Dad and began to fidget. There was something different about my father this day. I hadn't a clue what was going on as I sat obediently unsure where to look. An air of expectancy crept slowly into the room until it was almost too much to bear.

Dad suddenly frowned and began looking at me under his eyes which felt really weird. We must have sat there ten minutes, yet still nothing happening apart from the uneasy silence and awkward frowns. Again, he closed his eyes shaking his head as if plagued with torment and nodding his head repeatedly while telling himself no. To me, it looked like he was silently fighting against himself as a battle raged within him. To me, as a little girl sitting watching this it was horrendous. It was like there were two men in one man. At one point he was rocking and humming as he sat on the chair. He was in a world of his own and he didn't even realize I was there for moments.

Never in all my time in this house had I ever seen him acting so bizarre. So here I sat, alone in the early hours of the morning in our front room and I didn't understand this unusual behaviour coming from my dad. He hadn't done a thing to me yet, so I couldn't understand why my insides were erupting. The only sound apart from his mutterings was the sound of my heart beating in my ears. Minutes seemed like hours, and I tried desperately to understand what all this could mean.

I don't know why but a terrible, repulsive, sickening feeling rose through me. I wanted to move and get out of room, but I was frozen to the spot far too terrified to even bat an eyelid. I didn't know what to do or even why I was feeling this way.

I noticed tears rolling down my father's cheeks and in these intense and chilling moments the power of my uncertainty was over whelming to a point that I felt I might faint. Suddenly he began to softly sing to me, but it was almost as if it was not me he was seeing.

He sang, 'Far away across the waters lives an old German's daughter, on the banks of the old River Rhine. I loved her, I missed her, I had to leave her, my pretty, my pretty Fraulein, Fraulein, Fraulein…'

After a few minutes or so he opened his trousers. At that I turned away sharply, thinking he was drunk and had forgotten I was present. This was so unlike him, and I didn't particularly want to watch him piss in the fire grate. In-fact I was very embarrassed.

'Sally, don't turn away, look!' he said pulling something out of his trousers which puzzled me. I knew my little brothers had a thing like that however theirs were little and floppy, but his was big, straight, and nasty. It was ugly, so ugly. I imagined it being like a snake and it confused me. I didn't want to look but he made me which rose in me the most extreme vile mixtures of feeling I can never remember having before.

I remembered a very slight version of this feeling when the young man took me to the church steeple whilst in St Gerard's, but it was nothing in comparison to this.

I didn't know what he was doing but I knew it was rude to pull your knickers or your trousers down in front of someone. I sat trembling; desperately trying to summon up the courage to call for Mum but the words wouldn't come out of my mouth. I didn't know what to do, for I wasn't used to this, and Dad was being so rude. My discomfort got too much for me and I began to cry. I hated him for making me look. I was so embarrassed. I was becoming extremely distressed, but that didn't bother him at all as he asked, 'Sally, do you want to know what this is?'

'No Dad.'

'It's called a mickey.'

'Yes Dad, can I go to bed now please?'

'No. Come here and touch him. It's okay he won't hurt you, Sally.'

'No. No, I don't want to do that dad, I don't like it,' I began to back off and sob.

'Shut up and stop being stupid!' he barked. 'Now get over here and do what I tell you and now!'

My flesh crawled as I slowly walked towards him, knowing that there was no way out of whatever was about to happen. My heart sank as I was forced to submit myself to his will.

The air hung thick and heavy in the room. Stale cigarette smoke mixed with a pungent smell of alcohol which emanated from every pore of his putrid skin. Of course, I had no idea about sex. In fact, I had never heard of it, and I could not begin to work out what my father intended to do.

'Never mind thinking about it Sally,' he said with a faraway look in his eyes. 'Touch it and be quick about it girl.'

I began to shake as a sickening feeling rose through my gut and my hand trembled as I slowly brought it forward and touched it. On making contact I sharply pulled my hand back with disgust. Dad fixed his eyes on me and said, 'Hold it and hold it now girl.'

'No Dad, I can't. Please... I'

'Sally,' he warned.

His tone of voice made it clear that disobedience wasn't an option, so once again I brought my hand forward and taking a deep breath, I touched it again. It felt warm and sticky and every hair on my body felt like it was on end as my stomach lurched violently. He then began to order further sexual depravities from me.

'Now I want you to kiss it for me Sally.'

'No, no I won't. I just can't do that dad.'

'Oh, but you can and believe me you will. So, get on with it. Don't you make me ask you twice to do anything from now on. The minute I ask, you do. Have you got that?'

'OH, please don't do this to me Dad, please,' I begged as tears streamed down my face.

Ignoring my pleas, he pushed me down onto my knees, so my eyes were on the same level as his 'thing.' I drew back in horror at the sight of it so close. I looked up at my father with pleading eyes hoping he would remember I was just a little girl and his daughter, but my pitiful pleading gazes fell upon a merciless predator who was determined to have his wicked way. His eyes were wide like he was possessed with madness. His breaths were deep and heavy as he fixated on me with a look that would have turned lesser men's stomachs.

Oh, Jesus please help me, what can I do? I prayed inwardly. Tears flooded my face which must have fell on his thing, but there was to be no reprieve for me this day. One part of me knew that I had to obey but everything else in me screamed, *No!*

Dad grabbed me by the hair yanking my head forward with such ferocity that my lips smashed into his thing. A stench of stale urine thrust its way up my nostrils and I wretched as bile lined my throat. I tried desperately to free my hair from his grip, but it was no good. We were now engaged in a battle that only had one obvious outcome. My resistance only fuelled his rage and the harder I fought the harder he pushed my face into his thing. Then he began to rub it all over my face.

At that moment I wished I was dead. I closed my eyes tightly so at least I could not see what was happening, but I could feel the warm, sticky liquid which seeped from it slowly drying on my cheeks. I prayed that the house would fall down and kill me stone dead. I felt I could not live with the shame of this on my shoulders. I bit my lip to stop myself screaming out. But it was far from over. To my horror he started to pull my head forward once again and began to demand even more repulsive acts out of me.

I silently prayed for the courage for the nerve to bite it. I pictured myself opening my mouth and biting it so hard that my father would fall in agony screaming. He felt my continuous resistance which he did not like that at all, and he sharply pulled my face up to look into his eyes so I could smell his foul alcoholic breath, and said to me in a terrifying voice, 'Think you're clever now Sally? You've brought this on yourself.'

What happened next, happened on the settee. I lay silent fearing that he might kill me and bit my hand to help me get through this. It was so painful and disgusting that I remember crying aloud and his hand coming across my mouth. Then everything went black.

The next thing I recall it was like I was there, yet I wasn't there. I can't really explain it. It was like my mind had completely cut off and I was going the through the motions but was desensitized to it all. Then it all came flooding in - embarrassment, disgust, filth, hurt, humiliation, and a chilling tingling crept up my spine as all hell let loose in my head and I screamed out at him through gasps of pain, 'No more, Daddy please stop!'

Suddenly I felt a searing pain and in an utter sense of desolation I let out an unmerciful scream. The last thing I remember was my father covering my mouth again. After that my mind went blank and whether I fainted, or my mind was cast out I do not know.

I have searched into the darkest corners of my mind to recall the ending of that episode, but it has clearly gone. Whilst writing my life story I have recalled things which would seem impossible to remember as if I suddenly stepped back into the past. It is as if my mind refuses to shelter these festered memories anymore, but what happened on that settee next, I still do not know.

When I came to my senses, I was standing on my feet on a little green wooden box next to the front door which was the electric meter. Completely incoherent I looked about me for a moment as a sense of dim awareness came about me at the echo of voice slowly saying, 'It's alright Sally, you're alright. Sally, I'm sorry, please don't tell your Mum.'

Still far from my senses I looked about me as those words slowly rolled over in my mind. I began to feel something touching me below and looked down to see my father wiping me with a rag between my legs. Almost lifeless I looked back up and slowly looked about me again trying to fathom out what the heck had just happened and how on earth I'd ended up on this green wooden box. I felt dry and tried to swallow but I couldn't. My throat was too sore, and I couldn't even swallow the dryness away from my mouth.

Still staring in front of me I heard mumbling which seemed to be getting louder and louder and only then did the full features of my father focus clearly as he held my face in his hands and begged, 'Forgive me Sally. Please, I didn't want to do this. Oh Sally, I'm sorry Sally. Please speak to me Sal, say something come on girl, please!'

I opened and closed my mouth continuously trying to speak for him, but I couldn't. My mind began to wander as hundreds of thoughts flew through my brain until suddenly it came flooding back - the ugly reality of what had taken place in that room. But try as I might, I couldn't remember getting onto this box. I gasped with horror but still couldn't move or speak as my father lifted me into his arms and carried me into the kitchen.

'You'll be alright in a minute Sal, don't tell your mother on me please Sally. You won't tell her will you Sally?' He stood me onto the floor then and I nodded, 'No' in answer to him. This seemed to put him at ease a little and he then tried to please me a bit by saying, 'Do you want some corn beef Sal?' I shook my head and with great effort and managed to say in a weak, croaky voice, 'Drink.'

He gave me some milk and I tried to gulp it down but found it difficult to swallow. My mouth felt hard, my tongue crusty, and my throat began to burn as the milk slowly slid down.

'I'll make sure your mother lets you sleep in until you feel like getting up. Here's a shilling,' he said before going to bed.

Slowly I shuffled into the front room staring at the shilling in my shaking hand. Of course, I had no idea what it was all about then, but I knew that what had just happened was very wrong.

I began to feel a great disgust towards Jesus for forsaking me and letting this happen. Looking about at the squalor and filth I felt that he had forgotten me and left me to the fate of this poor and filthy house.

Surely that poor woman and the scruffy, rowdy children of whom I had grown to love can't really be my family and that wicked Pig whom I more than hate, can't really be my father, I reasoned. *Jesus has made a mistake putting me here. I'm not a part of this way of life; I should have been born into better. I don't want to be like these people.*

'I want my Aunty Gwen,' I sobbed. 'I need my Aunty Gwen. She's my Mummy really. Jesus why have you forsaken me?' The shilling was still in my hand. A cold, hard reminder of what had happened. 'You can shove this stinking shilling right up your arse Dad,' I boldly sobbed as I jumped off the chair and slung it across the room, before falling to my knees and sobbing and sobbing until I choked and vomited all over the grate.

CHAPTER 20

I found it hard to cope after my subjection to his sexually demoralizing depravity, and I withdrew fully into myself. I found it difficult to communicate with anybody, although I did, for I knew better than not to. The very sight of my Father made me tremble, and even though something within my gutsy little personality seemed broken, I was determined to survive.

So very much had happened to me by now which had obviously left its traumatizing scars. As they say, you can break a person's body, but you can never break their spirit- only He can do that.

At just ten-years-old I was practically running the house. For some while now it had become a regular occurrence for my folks to roll in after the night clubs in the early hours of the morning. All my siblings would be in bed apart from me, for I often dozed off on the settee with the huge iron door key tied around my neck ready to jump up fast and let my drunken parents in.

I was always last to bed and first up. Not to say I was woken from the little sleep I did get, to go down into the freezing cold, dark and creepy old kitchen to make the baby a bottle. There was no way my parents would get out of their cosy comfort zones to do it. I was so tired most of the time that I could hardly move, and many a time as I attended to the children, I would just burst into tears wanting to scream, 'Please let me sleep.' The children turned to me for almost everything and I did love them.

The housing department offered my mother another council house in the city and so we moved into our new home. Its wallpaper and paint were clean, and the kitchen floor had old red tiles and lino in the living-room. The stairs were bare floorboards – likewise in the bedrooms. However, apart from being a little dreary it was truly better than the last house and had its advantages, which were an extra bedroom and an attic. We also had a toilet right outside the back door which was brilliant! Maybe dad would use the loo now instead of peeing in the grate or sink and shitting in the cubby-hole.

At least this place was cleaner and brighter too. The terraced house stood between houses in a street full of houses on both sides of the road, unlike the back houses in the backdrop of the ghettos. This wasn't really a great area to live in either, but it still seemed nice enough to me. Although it mainly housed the working class, it was even in number in housing crooks, dole spongers and the emotional misfits of society. No wonder my parents loved the place - there was a pub on each end of our street. Halfway down the road in the middle of all the side-to-side houses, was a tiny shop. It was one of those old-fashioned grocery shops run by a very sweet middle-aged lady. It sold penny sweets or a bar of chocolate or toffee for three to six pence, bundles of firewood, coal, and all sorts of the food of the day.

It wasn't long before Mother began to get food and fags on the slate from her, reimbursing her each pay day. I hated it when the money ran out and one of us older kids would have to take a letter written by Dad to the shop asking for credit. The embarrassing thing was that even before the lady said yes, he had a written shopping list on the same page as the begging letter.

There was also a school over the road at the bottom of the street, which was a good thing seeing as Mother or Father never took the children there. Since I had lived with these people the kids had made their own way to school, even though this time they had to cross a main road to get to it.

Anyway, Mum decided that she liked this house and was really going to try to keep it clean and up to standard, which lasted for a very short while before the task was passed to me. There was always an excuse to drink, and the recent day's events made no difference. Most people might find it shattering after a house move. But not my parents – for them it was just another excuse to celebrate, so off they went on one of their many pub crawls to make themselves known in the local pubs.

Dad was known all over anyway. When you had been a boxer and had a reputation as a street brawler, people knew you or knew of you. I would think he thought people loved having him around these new pubs, but the truth was that most family men popping out for a quick pint felt a huge unease sharing a pub with such an unpredictable man.

On the first night in our new home my parents returned home about eleven fifteen, all cheery and very tipsy. They were accompanied by a couple from Belfast who lived just across the road. They were a bit older than my folk I would say, and the guy was a ginger nut. His wife was a strange one. She was a big girl with massive boobs. She had a massive amount of long, wavy, dyed black hair and wore a horrid thick, black eyeliner around her eye plus a blue shadow. Aiming for the Liz Taylor look I imagine. To accompany all that overuse of make-up, was some rouge and thick red lipstick, which I felt made her teeth look yellow.

To me she looked very silly. The children thought she was an old witch and were afraid of her, but I heard Mum privately telling my father she felt the lady looked more like an old whore or prostitute. Frankly I had no knowledge at all to what those two words meant.

Apparently, those people knew my father from the past and they now lived on the corner over the road with their ten children. So, in-fact they were our new neighbours and as time slipped by he became one of Dad's regular drinking partners and close friends. As the weeks flew by, their children and us children mingled together and paired off as friends; but we all played together. We older kids from both families had to take responsibility for our younger and baby siblings. So even in my play time which I rarely got, I was working. It was a scream when we all went out together which was daily for a few weeks.

There were at least twenty kiddies roaming about together. I would push a huge pram with the twin boys strapped in, and woe-be-tide me if one fell out or got hurt. We were a sight to behold as we all trotted off to the park, and once we got fed-up there, off we all rambled over to the bomb-peck to have a blast. This place was so dangerous but for us it was an amazing place to be and full of excitement.

My newfound freedom was short lived with my father s interruption one day, as I was on my way out of the door with my siblings, 'You've had your fun now it's back to the old routine.' I knew full well what every word of that meant.

His drinking was worse than ever, the new house was a pig sty, and mum and I caught the after wave of dad's bad moods. He began to kick ten tons of shit out of us. I was not allowed to go to school because of the horrific physical states he often left me in.

I don't know what happened to the Social Workers for a while. I think it was that my parents did the same old trick of leaving a house and telling no-one where they had gone. It took a few months, but the authorities eventually tracked us down, or fresh complaints from neighbours reporting child abuse alerted them to the family. In this case I believe the latter may have been the case.

The more he drank the more delusional he was and the deeper he sank into alcohol induced psychosis. His antics became shocking. I wasn't allowed to mix with his children again. So, unless I was babysitting, skiving after everybody, or being a human out-let for my father to vent his rage on, I was banished to the attic (unless I was summoned to make an appearance when I was wanted or needed.) The attic consisted of floorboards, bare walls and an old army metal single bed which had a dirty bare mattress and old coats for blankets.

I'd stand on the bed so I could reach the window and gaze out in tears as my ears were filled with the endless screams of excitement and laughter of my family and friends whom I missed more than anything now. One little boy always gazed at our attic and would stand with his hands in his pockets looking up at me sadly for a moment then he would wave and give me a smile.

I was allowed down at night to take care of the kids and often my sister and I had to go up and lie with them until they fell asleep. More than ever before both my parents began staying out all night leaving me, a ten-year-old kid responsible for anything. The first time it happened we all slept together in my siblings' double bed.

Sally was our boxer dog who belonged to Dad, so at least on their many all-nighters we had her company for she was a good deterrent. I really felt sorry for the dog. She was having pups and of course when she was almost ready to have them, there were some unpleasant sights about the dog as she walked about. When Dad was drunk, oh my, he was so cruel to Sally. He booted her straight up the backside and really abused the beautiful animal.

As soon as they'd go out, I hurried to sit with Sally and hug her and she always came to me. It was like we shared that common bond - that in our suffering we were inexplicably linked. He had had Sally since a pup and even though she tried to growl at him when he started on me, as soon as he ran at her, she cowardly ran to hide. It wasn't her fault - she was as terrified of him as I was. Yet, what I found very strange was that when the dog went into labour Dad lay down in the kitchen with her all night helping her bring her pups into the world. Dad was so kind to her and as gentle as a lamb.

We spent many a day without a bite to eat. I had got used to the constant hunger pangs, but one thing I couldn't cope with was the twins going without their milk. They'd look at me with pleading eyes while they screamed continuously for a bottle. Of course, this was too much. I had to do something.

So, early in the mornings I got up, waited until the milkman had dropped the milk on someone's step and then out, I would pop and nick at least four bottles from different doors. I always took a few carrier bags with me or my sister to help. If I was lucky, as well as the milk I would get a loaf, eggs and butter in my bag, then back to the house to the warm the milk and make the feed for the kiddies.

In our house for about four days after pay day we got fed, then as the week come to an end, it got less and less. So, unless Mum could borrow some money or get some credit from the shop – which more than often she did, my sister and I would try and nick some food anyway and anywhere we could.

I remember once us trotting along the road like a little pair of tramps until we came across a shop which looked like a small supermarket. We walked in slowly clutching hands as we looked about us continuously to make sure nobody was watching us. We took a long and careful look before suddenly grabbing whatever we could and slinging it into our bag. Leaving a trail of stuff behind us which we had dropped, we legged it out of the door, and from that day to this it still puzzles me how we never got caught.

After that we found a café which was just up the road to burgle. Our back yard was being dug up so all the pipes could be fixed and one night playing in the manhole out-side our back door, I noticed a light shining up at us. We went and got Dad who realized it was a hatch into what seemed to be the roof of the store house at the back of the cafe.

Dad took our arms and lowered my sister and I down into the food store. We started stealing the food and passed it up to him. There were big blocks of butter and cheese, bread, tea and massive tins of beans and tomatoes. There were loads of meat, potatoes and cakes, biscuits and so many goodies. For a few weeks we emptied that place, and I was always confused to why it took them so long to find out their business was being cleaned out. I can only imagine they may have gone on holiday or something. One night we went to rob it again and it was all boarded up. The game was up.

My father's paranoid thinking regarding me became worse. Sally was always the bad one. Apparently, I was going to grow up and show him up by marrying a black man. Oh, the other girls were fine. They would grow up and marry good men who would take care of them, our mother and him when they got old.

His boys? Well Dad had plans for their lives too. He couldn't seem to cope with his own life, but nevertheless he had plans for his son's lives. This one was obvious; they were going to be boxers, and good street fighters at that – but when it came to me! Depending on the day and his mood, oh, he was sure I would turn out to be a lesbian or a prostitute. Well, he certainly had high hopes for me, seeing I was going to be a lesbian that married a black man who turned me into a prostitute.

CHAPTER 21

Many times, my father made the effort to try and stop drinking but to little avail. It always lasted a few days or at the longest, a few weeks. Looking back now, I guess I can recognize the endless struggle he suffered - almost as if he couldn't live with the drink and he couldn't live without it. Once he put the drink down, he was sick and spent a day or so in bed. Then he would sit around the house, almost in silence, very agitated and always criticising the state of the place which put Mum on eggshells. Although I jumped about skivvying after him, he didn't physically hurt me in these times, so it was okay by me.

I think the longest I may remember him lasting off the booze was a couple of months and boy did life change for the better in that time. We ate a lot because we had a lot more money, all around the house was spotless and I was allowed to have more fun like my siblings. When Dad was dry, Mum was dry, and she would cook lovely big pots of Irish strews.

I recall getting up early one morning, only to see my father already up. He had tidied the house and was sitting alone in the front room. When I saw him, my face must have given away my inner fear because he looked at me in horror and told me to sit down, 'Sally, you're pale- what's the matter? I'm not going to hurt you kid.'

'I know Dad. I'm alright.'

'Good God, you're full of fear and I've done this to you. I don't want you living in fear like this Sally. Sal, I'm trying, I never meant to do what I did - it's that demon drink. It makes a monster out of ya.'

'It's okay Dad. Do you want a cup of tea,' I said getting up. This sort of kind talk from Dad for some reason made me uncomfortable. I guess I had grown so used to his barbaric behaviour that I was at a loss how to cope when he was trying to be caring. The truth was that I didn't trust him and after years of endless broken promises and brutal tantrums, I was unsure of everything anymore. So, I learned very quickly over the years that to survive and cope in these savage surroundings meant that I would have to take every day as it comes. Now that he was making a serious attempt to free himself from his demons, I guess I had to try and get in line with him and start living my life, one day at a time.

Behind his back, Mum said he was having a mental break-down and referred to the fact that he was mentally ill. I mean if they had words, I often heard her saying he was 'bleeding mental.' She found it hard to cope with the change even though it was much easier for us all. Mum felt that when dad was off the gargle, he was a 'Fooking nutter.'

However, I felt it was the best I had ever seen him, and he was a much nicer human being for it. The truth was, he noticed a lot more about the way things were run in the house - the filth of the place, Mum's past drinking - but what really offended her was when he said that I was doing too much and had too much to cope with.

He told her that she needed to look after the kids, and he would try and help but it was time Sally started to attend school and was allowed the right to be a kid. He also felt I had been through the mill, and it was time I got treated like the rest of his kids.

'She's my kid too and our first born,' I heard him say one day.

Those words rang through my head for he had never admitted that before and I wondered who in-fact I did belong too. He was calling me 'his kid' and for the first time those words gave me a sense of belonging. Just maybe this man might be a nice guy and really did love me deep down.

The strange thing was that as my father began to pay attention to me and treat me kindly as he did his other children, my mother began to find fault in all I did, even continually telling him tales on me. Not for specifically anything I had done wrong, but for accidently dropping a bottle of milk. For when dad was on the piss, there was no such a thing as an accident. I'd messed up and that was it.

Mum would say things like, 'I had to call her three times to come in Paddy.' Silly little things like that. If I didn't clean under the beds to her liking, she would belt me over the head with a sweeping brush or get mad and after slapping me across the face try to bite me with her gums. Sometimes she would pull me around the bedroom by my hair. Boy that hurt. Yet somehow, I would sort of hold the parts of my body she had hurt, going 'oochhh!' in an un-cheeky manner.

I never trembled with her as I did when Dad even called me in anger. She seemed to get really upset with me for the most trivial of things. One would have thought she would have been delighted my dad was making an effort to get to know me and trying to act like my father, but no, she seemed to be resentful because sadly, she was jealous.

When he was sober my father liked the fact that I realised he had been sick. He felt that I had a slight understanding that he personally did not want to hurt me like that but when the demon drink took over and made him sick, he did things that he would never dream of doing when sober. He used to say that I was the clever one. A very clever kid and I would go a long way in life if I could get to school more.

Despite everything, when he was sober, I admired him, respected him, and loved him a little. It was like living with a different person - such a far cry from a few months before where I hated my days and dreaded the nights. These days, although not perfect I couldn't complain. They were better than I had ever experienced at home and at least now he treated me the same as his other kids.

However, I guess all good things come to an end and to our horror Dad went missing one afternoon and Mum was getting a bit concerned. I didn't know what to expect if he happened to be drinking again, for I was sure after our few months together of late we'd most likely be fine. After all, he now acknowledged me as his own. In saying that, drink usually meant Dad became a cold hearted callous cruel individual, who caused chaos in the home as he continuously went berserk. So that horrible gut-rending uneasiness returned, robbing me of my newfound peace and changing my world up-side-down.

So, lying in bed this particular night, I only had to hear his footsteps walking up the street and I know by the sound of the steel caps that he was drunk. I began to tremble from head to toe then and very quickly hid under the blankets snuggling down, hoping not to get noticed amongst my siblings. No such luck, for as usual in these same circumstances he pulled back the blankets and giving me the evil eye for a moment said, 'Up you little Bastard - say goodbye to the Mr nice guy and get over here. Stand to attention until I tell you to move Scab!'

Then he turned his attention to Mum also lying in bed.

'Is this what you f***ing wanted women? Is it?' She started to get out of bed as though she wanted to try and get him into it, and I felt now that she was regretting the protest she put up against our new life when he was dry.

'For f*** sake Paddy don't start! You'll wake the kids, come, and get into bed.'

Out of nowhere he gave her such a punch in the face that she fell back on the bed as blood burst everywhere and knocked her out cold.

'Pleased with yourself now you dirty whore?' he shouted at her unconscious figure.

Getting no response, he suddenly turned to me and lashed the sharpest back-hander across my face which knocked me flying across the room. I heard my siblings screaming and begging him to stop but he ignored their pitiful pleas as though he couldn't hear them. Another sudden punch to the head and to the face knocked me to the ground and after yet more obligatory beatings for Mother and me, he suddenly began to calm the kids down then moved Mum over covered her up and got into bed telling me, 'You lie on the floor Scab. Don't let me see you in that bed with my kids.'

Silently I sobbed as I lay on the freezing floorboards of the bedroom all night with my head throbbing. I was in agony and couldn't open one eye. My forehead was swollen, and my face was black and blue. I was a sorrowful sight in a pitiful condition without a friend in the world, with no escape from my ordeal.

At times I drifted into an uneasy sleep only to be plagued with dreams of my Father chasing me. When I awoke, I was forced to wait until he woke and gave me permission to move. I wasn't allowed to even go to the toilet - which in our house was the shit bucket on the landing, so unfortunately, I wet myself.

The next morning Mother took the children downstairs and left me lying on the floor. When I opened my eyes to the realization of the previous night's antics, I was broken hearted and bitterly disappointed and began wishing for God to help me. *He never did so why should he now?* I thought bitterly. Maybe Sister Brendon and Aunty Gwen were wrong, and my father was right after-all, and there really wasn't a God for if there was, I couldn't understand why he allowed me to suffer so.

I hoped that when Dad decided to wake, he might regret his actions and put the drink down again. There I was again expecting too much from those who could give nothing. When he eventually woke, I noticed him glaring at me, so I kept observing him through the corner of my eye because I didn't want to look directly eye to eye with him. He just kept starring before ordering me to stand beside his bed. He then looked me in the eyes, put his hand into my pants and started to fumble about with me. I felt sick as my body shook with hate and disgust and I despised him for making me stand here and take this. He just kept on mauling me which made me cringe to the bone, repulsing me with his every touch.

I knew what this was all about now and the perverseness of it all made my skin crawl. I was degraded and defeated – demoralized and depleted and you might think it must stop here for surely no-one can go on suffering like this, but I could, and I did.

The Social Services popped in and out keeping an eye on us, but they must have been using the eyes of a blind man, for so many unacceptable things were going on right under their noses that they simply did not pick up on. Many years later I was stunned to hear a Social Service report once read, 'The home is very poor but spotlessly clean.' Well, it would be, for if they came unannounced, they never got in, and then Mum knew they would be back, so I helped her scrub the place clean.

Life was a nightmare once again and just when I thought Dad couldn't do anything more to hurt me or shock me, he came up with another party trick. I was sleeping in the attic one night when he came to my room and ordered me out of bed to stand to attention in front of him. As I did, he raised a machete knife and swung it past my head, telling me that if I moved my head was coming off. The fear of God overtook me, until my whole body began to tremble and even my head shook in fright. Drips of water slowly puddled between my legs as I wet myself.

When he tired himself of that he dragged me off to the long metal gas pipe which stood out of the ground in the fire grate of the attic, then the lunatic, with no regard for his other sleeping children and wife below, switched the gas on and made me breath it in a few seconds at a time, until he felt I had learned my lesson.

Another punishment that I had to endure of his making was what he did with the knowledge that I was terrified of heights. Late of a night when the household and neighbours slept, he would come to the attic, wake me, open the window, and hang me right out of the window holding me by the ankles.

'I can drop you any time I choose Scab and we would say you must have jumped out of the window,' he told me. I was terrified of heights, so I closed my eyes trying not to look down. Several times, I almost drowned as I vomited with fright and the fluid flew back into my face and up my nose.

It didn't take him long to pull me back in the window after that. After all he didn't want anybody to hear me coughing and choking outside, for how could he explain away his daughter hanging out of the attic window as somebody dangled her by her ankles? No, that wouldn't suit my father at all, for he was a pub angel and a house devil. No, being caught in the act would do at all.

Father was very good at intimidating and terrorizing his family but when he had to face professionals to explain the physical evidence left on my person through his brutal assaults, he always went on the missing list leaving mother to face the music.

CHAPTER 22

It wasn't long before the Social Security finally caught up with my mother. They turned up at the house one morning unannounced because somebody had reported her for co-habiting with Dad. My parents were out of their deceitful comfort zones now and as you may imagine, Dad hid while Mum stuttered her way through the questioning. Her stammer had got much better since she married my father, and she was brilliant at pulling that rabbit out of the hat when it was convenient.

There was a box of ten cigarettes on the table and the Social Security Officer was not shy in asking her straight out, 'If you're struggling as much as you say you are Mrs Murphy, why are you buying these? Is this not taking food out of your children's mouth?' holding the fags up in his hands for her to see his disapproval.

She wasn't as dumb as Dad accused her of being when he was pissed, for she had an answer for everything the social security officer asked her. When he had written down her statement, she put her mark on it and off he went leaving her in no doubt that he didn't believe a word she was saying. Had the decision of this claim been left up to him, he would have stopped her money and closed her claim immediately.

As he walked out of the door he sarcastically said, 'There's no smoke without fire!' To which she replied, 'Good bleeding job it's not left up to you to starve me and the kids then isn't it!'

You see, we can fool some of the people some of the time, but we can't fool all of the people all of the time. Because they were now watching our home, to my utter joy my father had to leave the family home for a while. Once he was gone the atmosphere became far more relaxed. I was left in charge again to cater for all of us which I did to the best of my ability. Dad went to live in a pokey little room in Balsall Heath, which was rented by a couple of friends of his.

Mum appearing to be unable to live without him, went to see him every day at first. Sometimes she was gone all night but as time went by, her time with him got less as he would remind her, she needed to get home and spend some time with her kids. So, every day turned into every few days.

One day, out of the blue the guy next door came and asked my mother had she seen his wife. She was a nice lady who often had a cuppa or a drink with Mum and Dad, but her husband pretty much kept to himself. Evidently, she had left home a few days after my father had left home. My mother knowing that my father was a whore master had a really bad feeling about this and decided to be her own private eye in her mission to discover the truth.

Once she returned from being with Dad, she never returned for a few days as they had an arrangement when to meet so father wouldn't go missing on the booze. This time however, although she had returned home, she was very ill at ease as she endlessly paced the living room.

It must have been around 9.30pm that night after she had drunk her two large bottles of Guinness when she told me to get ready. Off we went on the bus to where he was living, in search of my Father. Without a second thought she marched in and went straight upstairs to the lodging very quietly. We stood in the shadows of the landing while she waited the return of the folks who lived in the room.

She was so agitated she kept whispering to me, 'I swear to God I'll burst her f***ing face wide open if I catch her with him!'

All too soon the folks returned from the pub and as soon as they opened their door and entered the room, before they even had time to close it after them, she came out of no-where and booted the door straight out of their hands, shocking the life out of everyone including my father. As she hurried into the room, she caught him red handed in bed with the woman from next door.

I was mortified firstly at what Mum had done and now at the adultery that openly greeted my eyes. There was no stopping Mum though and she went berserk. First, she dragged the lady by the hair out of the bed and around the room. Then she took her shoe off and slung it at Dad in the bed. She ran over to him and full of rage started to belt him over the head with her shoe. She must have taken leave of her senses because the fact that he might batter her to death for this didn't bother her at all. She was far too angry to care.

While Mother was clobbering Father, the woman got dressed and grasped the opportunity to sneak off but Mum catching that through the corner of her eye was hot on her heels. She grabbed her long hair from the back of her head and all bedlam let lose. My mother was determined to teach her a thing or two and furiously beat her around the street.

Mum couldn't have been taller than 5ft 3inchs but by gum she could take care of herself. She'd fought the biggest and the best of women fist to fist in her time.

It was manic and noisy as the two women persisted to try and knock the block off each other. Mum punched her to the ground and dragged her into the road. Cars stopped and a bus skidded just in front of them as traffic came to a sudden halt. Drivers shouted, some even got out to look, while others honked their horns endlessly.

By now my father had joined us and stood beside me watching the action, making sure none of the guys interfered while the two women were brawling - not a hope of him trying to stop it. The woman screamed as she lay in the road trying to cover her face which was covered in blood. Regardless of that there was no stopping mum. She was furious. She booted her to the ribs, tummy and head and each time she lashed a boot she verbally abused her, 'Take that for running off with that dirty no good whore master I'm unfortunately married to, you nasty slut!'

Mum's rival curled up on the ground in a ball of agony holding her stomach as she screamed to my father to help her. I couldn't help but feel sorry for her; this was a frenzied attack which really needed to be stopped now for Mum was going too far.

'For God's sake, help me, Paddy!' screamed the poor woman.

My Mother stopped after hearing that. Turning to my father she shouted mockingly, 'Come on Paddy, come and save your little whore!' Then she took her shoe off again and fuelled all her rage into hitting the woman over the head with it.

Mum was so angry at the fact this was her neighbour and friend. She felt that she had taken her for a right fool. Living right next door this woman knew what a bastard Dad was and how he treated my mother. Many a night she must have heard the desperate screams of my mother as my father beat her about the house. There is no way she could not hear seeing that her house was attached to ours and the walls were like paper. Mother had even cried to her over a cup of tea with her two black eyes and battered face and she had often told Mum to get the police and get him out or to leave.

But Mum's answer was always the same, 'Where could I go with nine children? Who would offer me refuge?' Plus, the police don't get too involved with domestic violence, so what could she do? No-one had any answer to that, so she felt she had to stay.

The truth was that if Mum had got a wonderful opportunity to get herself and us children into a place of safety and comfort, I doubt very much if she would have gone. Awful as my father was, she was crazy about him. One minute she loved him the next minute she hated him. It was a sure case of she couldn't live with him, but she couldn't live without him either.

Now this woman from next door was so different. I can't help but wonder what was on her mind. She had a wonderful hard-working husband and three beautiful sons. She was an attractive, well-dressed lady who kept a clean and modern home.

Dad may have been a smartly dressed, handsome man with a reputation as a tough guy but there was a huge but in this - he hadn't a penny to his name. He rarely worked, he was a bum that drank the food out of kid's mouths, a wife beater, a child abuser, and a paedophile. Dear me, this lady had some taste in men.

Many abusers are known to be very charming at first - otherwise how on earth could they attract women? For this lady to think he would leave Mum, stay with her and change was sheer madness! If he did leave Mum to live with her, why wouldn't he start doing to her want he did to us? Personally, I was sold out on the idea of him running off with her and leaving us.

Yet I must admit, my father got more involved with this woman than he ever had with any of his lovers before. He was truly going to leave Mum for good to set up home with her, but he kept saying he wanted his kids to live with them. She agreed to that at first until she realised it was not going to be all wine and roses living with Paddy Murphy's children.

Plus, after meeting up with her husband for a talk, she felt she couldn't do this to her kids or family. She decided that she wouldn't mind continuing to see Dad, but she wasn't prepared to do much more. To my amazement he agreed to that and if Mum wanted to keep him in her life, she was going to have to accept it and share him. I was stunned that my mother tolerated this. We were young but we understood much and when Mum was alone, she cried to me about her pain surrounding it.

Dad struggled as he watched Mother beating up his lover of the moment - but he never interfered when two women fought. It was the fear of my mother getting herself arrested which made me go over and beg her to stop. If it wasn't for that, I truly believe that she'd have left her for dead.

Then my father did something that neither of us expected. He went to his lover's aid and helping her up off the ground and promptly ran off down the street with her hand in hand. My mother was stunned, and I was so shocked that if this hadn't been so obviously painful for Mum, I would have fell in the gutter pissing my-self laughing.

CHAPTER 23

A few weeks later Dad sent a message to the house asking my mother to meet him in the pub that night. I hoped that pride might stop her from going but true to form, she went. At about half past eleven my father, Mother and Shirley, his lover, returned home laughing amongst themselves, seemingly utterly enjoying each other's company. Dad carried a large tin of sweets for us kids.

The children were still awake and hearing their father's voice, ran downstairs shouting merrily welcoming him. He sat down as they gathered around him, and he gave them handfuls of sweets as they all chatted away excitedly, thrilled to see their father. The kids really loved Dad and rightly so too as he never harmed a hair on their heads, for he loved and adored them.

'They're fine children Paddy. No wonder you're proud of them,' said Shirley from next door.

Mum smiled at her, and I couldn't get to grips with these three all being nice to each other. However, I was convinced this would be short lived and all end in tears, for as much as Mum was being pleasant and agreeable this night, I knew that a great part of this was because her husband had returned home. I knew the shit would hit the fan before too long.

After dad had enjoyed his children, he suddenly turned his attention to me. As usual when Dad was around, I sat away from his children alone in a corner, like the odd one out.

'Come over and get some sweets Sal, don't sit over there on your own.'

I couldn't believe his caring kind tone and was sure it was to impress Shirley. However, that bothered me little right now. At least I didn't need to fear tonight. I could try and relax and enjoy this attention. Cautiously, I went over and took some sweets, thanking him as I went and sat down again close by.

'My little Sarah is that one, aren't you?'

Yes Dad,' I replied, rather surprised to hear him call me Sarah and liking it a little. He very rarely called me this and only when he was pleased with me.

'You like being called Sarah, don't you?'

'Yes Dad, but I've got to like Sally now. I'm used to it.'

'Come over here and sit by your old Dad for a minute Sally.'

I did that, feeling a little uncomfortable as I sat close to him, but I was not frightened as I knew that he was not going to hurt me that night.

'Sarah means Princess in Arabic,' he told me. 'She was the mother of the Jews. Did you know that, Sally?'

'No Dad I didn't!'

'Sarah was my mother's name you know Sally?'

'I didn't know that, Dad!' I replied. *I bet she wasn't called Scabby* I thought to myself. Shortly after I got up to make them a cup of tea, but I could still hear them chatting away from the kitchen.

'My mother was a lady and a very clever woman,' Dad said.

'I know she was Paddy,' replied my mother.

'Sally is like my mother. She's a little lady and very clever for her age. I'm wicked to that kid. Her nerves are in a terrible state and I'm holding her back from school. She's got to get to school. She has a good brain in her head that one and will go far one day - as strong as a lion – a born survivor. Sally's a leader among men - never forget that Mother.'

'I know she is Paddy and I love her as well.'

'It's sad about her leg,' said the woman next door. 'But she's a pretty child. You have a right to be proud of her.'

'Oh, there're no worries with her leg,' my father said. 'She's clever and a good-looking kid. She'll cop a good stroke in life that one, one day.'

'Anybody would think you were dying Paddy!' my mother said. 'What's wrong with ya? You're talking as though you're a dying man!'

'I'm not Maria, I'm being realistic.' There was an embarrassing silence. 'I'm a fighter and one day I'll get it,' said Dad. 'And when I do, listen to Sally because she'll be the backbone of this family - mark my words.'

I busied myself making their mugs of tea and was utterly moved by my father's words. He was such a different character when he was like this. I could only presume he was happy at this minute, that this lady, Shirley, made him happy. She must have done something that my mother couldn't do because he adored her. I quite liked her actually, she used to give the children and myself a cup of Oxo and peas with bread outside her back door in the past and we loved it. Had Mum known we liked her so much she would have gone ape shit.

That night after we all went to bed my sister and I heard a lot of giggling coming from my parent's room. In-fact it woke us in the night. She had nerves of steel and whispered, 'Come on.'

We sneaked up as though we were going to use the disgusting piss and shit bucket on the stairs and oh my goodness! My little sister began to listen at the door. To our surprise we then heard three voices in the room and obviously in the bed - Mum, Dad, and Shirley.

'Sal, quick listen to this! It's her next door in bed with Mum and Dad!'

Suddenly Dad shouted, 'Who's that?'
My sister, having balls of steel opened their bedroom door very quickly and said smiling, 'It's only us dad!' and she caught the three of them in bed together.

'Never come in without knocking again now go to bed,' he said. She returned to our bed giggling, 'When did Dad ever care if we knocked Sal? They're all in bed together. I think they're doing sex.'

We knew the noises so well considering that we heard it often when we all slept in their bedroom. It often happened when they presumed we were all sleeping. The sound had woken me, and it made me feel so uncomfortable.

The next morning Mum found it hard to look my sister in the eye at first, but my sister came straight out with it and asked Dad why Shirley was in bed with him and Mum. He told her she was dreaming so it would be wrong to repeat that to anyone. She agreed with him, promising to never mention it again and as she came to me smiling, she said, 'He must think I am stupid Sal.'

Apart from that, up until now where I am blowing the whistle on it she never told a soul and our parent's kinkiness was a family secret. The woman next door inevitably went back to her husband and things settled down. This upset my father a bit, but I am sure it was more about pride then a broken heart for it didn't take him long to get over her.

It wasn't long before Dad hit the bottle again and very heavily. He didn't need an excuse, but Dad always found one. Now and again gargled out of his mind he would reminisce about Shirley to Mum. Good Lord, how foolish was he. Mum would go nuts and it wasn't too long before he found very few nice things to say about anyone.

These days as he returned home, he also started to insult and abuse the neighbours - including Shirley next door. You would see lights go off and curtains twitch as he came drunk up the road. His resentment towards people was amazing; I don't think he even knew why he was starting on them. He was a public nuisance that thrived on intimating and bullying decent folk - a major pain in the arse that affected the whole street. Most people wondered who he was going to slag off publicly next.

He started to public name call which was so childish. My Mum secretly loved this and did her best to egg him on and encouraged him to insult Shirley publicly, which sadly he did. He'd stand outside her door calling her dirty whore and dirty knickers.

I couldn't help but think, *what a guy - what a gentleman?* Every bit of this man repulsed me. Of course, it wasn't long before this all rubbed off on me and I suffered terribly each time he returned home drunk. My nerves were in tatters as I was subject to his never-ending violence but that was not good enough for Dad. It seemed he wanted me to suffer the same anguish and torment as he was and before leaving the house for his drinking spree each day, he left me under constant threat of what was sure to happen to me on his return.

There was no relaxation for me. Day and night, I lived in constant fear of what was to happen on his return or sobbing in pain while it was happening. There was no let-up, no relief, no respite, no mercy, and no way out. I was trapped - doomed to be slaughtered by this evil man I was sure - I just didn't know the day or the hour this would happen, but I felt it was close. He made it clear that I would die at his hands and that where he put me no one would ever find me. He said I would never ever get away from him, that there was nowhere to run and nowhere for me to hide. He said even if he died, he would still get me. He said I would never get rest from him for he would haunt me, and I believed him.

It wasn't long before Mother went and got herself pregnant again with her ninth child. I knew it was just another responsibility for me and although I loved all my little brothers and sisters, it was murder trying to keep the house clean and in order. Not to say mothering all of my little family twenty-four hours a day and grabbing only a few hours' sleep when I could. Father was out drinking day and night, and Mum joined him a lot of a nights at this point.

Then of course there were the nights they went off to the night club after the pubs had closed, which was a four o'clock in the morning wake up call for me. Adding to that my parents stayed out all night many a time and at times we wouldn't see them for two or three days. Where were the Social Services many might think? Well, they often knocked but we rarely saw them. In fact, they knocked lots of times on evenings or mornings when Mother was out and had left us alone, but we knew the ropes, complete silence and pretend no one is in. Now and again, they would knock next door asking when they last saw us or heard us and they were told to our horror, 'We heard the children running around and shouting a few minutes ago and I haven't seen them go out.'

They'd come back then banging on the door and shouting through the letterbox, 'Sally, open the door, there's a good girl – come on Sarah we know you're in there!' Again, we stayed very silent until they left.

As soon as my parents returned and heard Dad said he couldn't be found in the home due to the Social Security, which was a load of cobblers. He simply didn't want to face the shame of their questions or be attached to the neglect of the children and the shame of our poverty stricken home he subjected his family to live in. What a waste of space he was!

I never wanted to be as emotionally pathetic as I felt my mother was with a man when I got older. He not only abused her, degraded her, humiliated her and disrespected her - he treated her like dirt and walked all over her. He used to say in jest to her, 'Women are like carpets, lay them properly the first time and you can walk all over them for life'.

What a male chauvinist pig he was and Mum putting up with it was beyond me. Even as a young girl I found it offensive and wondered where her self-respect was. I was determined when I got older that no man was ever going to even think he could get away with thinking I would tolerate any messing about by him.

To be fair, Mum didn't often drink in the day but when she went on drinking sprees who knew when she might come home. She took the alcohol and then the alcohol took her wherever she needed to be to get a drink. On the rare occasion that I did have some time to myself, Mum would use that time to bounce all her problems off me. I lived from day to day on the edge of a cliff, pure fear propelling me on, holding me back from teetering over the edge.

Mother got complications in the fifth month of her pregnancy and was hospitalised for her own mental and physical health. She knew full well that her absence gave my Father full reign to do whatever he wanted to me. He continued to tie me up by the feet with rope or flex wire and hang me upside down on the door and this began to happen day after day. The children would walk past me as if it was normal to have a sibling hanging like a bat on the kitchen door or the landing.

CHAPTER 24

I had laboured to keep this family together, trying to look after everybody and protect my parents even though there was no gratitude which I really did not expect, but the continuance of father's noxious behaviours and brutality was now more than anyone could expect me to endure. What he had done to me was despicable and I was at my wits end. Apart from killing me I could not see what else he might inflict on me, so I decided to run away yet again.

I did and I was missing all day until somebody spotted me, and I was picked up by the police and taken to a police station whereby it seems I was listed as missing. When I arrived at the police station I was put into a room for a short time. It was a dull room with a morbid atmosphere and looked rather like a cell I suppose. The dingy cream paint flaked off the bricked walls. A table and two chairs stood on a black concrete floor underneath a barred up small window. It was dimly lit and presented a cold, rugged, hostile sort of environment that matched the winter weather outside.

I was tired and very, very frightened knowing that when I returned the monster would get me. Maybe not this night but as soon as the police stopped investigating my allegations and the Social Services had been and gone, boy was I for it.

Eventually a police officer came in. To my joy they did not seem to realize I was missing and asked me, 'Will you tell us your surname and where you live?'

'Sorry Sir, I can't.'

'Why not Sally?'

'Because if I do you will send me home, and if you do that my dad will kill me.'

They went out and came back with a female police officer and asked me could I show them where my father was hurting me. I showed them the belt marks on my back and backside and pinch and bite marks on my hands, arms, and tops of my legs.

They left the room and came back with yet another police officer who asked gently, 'How did you get all these marks on you Sally?' as they examined my face, head, hands, back and legs. He told me that he was a Daddy and could he look at my backside.

'I've already told the other policeman before Sir.'

'Yes, I know that dear, but you must tell me as well and if you're asked again by other policemen, you must tell them as well.'

'My Dad did it Sir.'

He wanted details and I was only too happy to oblige. I don't know why but the floodgates opened, and I told him everything about my beatings.

'Come on Sally, where do you live?' But that was one piece of information I wasn't prepared to give. I thought by doing that it would take them weeks to find out where I was from. Little did I know that all it took was a phone call to the main police station in Birmingham and they knew! For I had been reported missing.

Again, they left the room for a moment and shortly after, the police-lady returned asking me would I let her see my backside. I hesitated for a moment before agreeing and letting her see my bum. After looking, she left the room for a moment before returning and asking me, 'Sally, will you let the sergeant look at your backside for me?'

It was like an every-one wants to peep at my bum game. It took a little coaxing but eventually I agreed. I mean, I was unsure how many police officers had peeped at my bum by now. With that they took me into another room and covered me up in some coats and told me to rest. But sleep wasn't on the agenda.

I listened as the police lady asked the Sergeant could she take me home for the night until the Social Services were called in the morning. None of the police were comfortable with what they could see on my body, but I was not of their jurisdiction, so I had to be taken back to my Police Station. When they arrived to collect me the reality of my position hit me, and I knew that I was going to go home before the night was out.

To this day I don't know how I managed to get out of that police station without getting caught, but I did. I simply sneaked down the passage and out of the door then ran up the road. Running along through the dark, freezing night was terribly frightening and my foot was killing me. I managed to hide in a nearby greenhouse, but it wasn't long before they found me, and I gave in to the fact that I was going home.

Arriving at Steel House Lane Police station, I was taken into a room and asked many questions by different police officers who looked at the evidence on my body. Shortly after my mother was brought into the room and we were left for a moment. She looked so sad and tired as she sat, very pregnant and pleaded with me, 'Don't do this to me Sally. Not yet kid. I'm just not strong enough to take it. Tell them the kids did it to you. Please Sally. Say you said it because you wanted to go back to the hospital. Stick by me Sally, please, I'm begging ya.' She began to cry desperately, and I was filled with pity for her. I felt I couldn't put her through anymore as she was having the baby, so when the police officer returned, I stuck by her, but he did not believe a word of it, 'Okay Mrs Murphy, tell us what happened to Sally.'

'The kids keep belting her with belts and sticks. She only says all that because she wants to get back to the hospital.'

'Why should she say that Mrs Murphy? Surely if she's happy at home she wouldn't keep running off like this?'

'I don't know, she's like that, our Sally.'

'Why don't you stop the other children beating her like that then Mrs Murphy? Sally has some very serious marks on her body, and I can't believe it has been inflicted by her siblings.'
'I wasn't in, that's why,' she said digging herself a hole to crawl out of.

'Come on Mrs Murphy we know Paddy did it. If he not beating you, he's beating her. Put him away and give yourself and the children a break. We'll go and take him right now and he won't have a chance to hurt you all again. Give him up to us, if not for you, think of your child. We are going to look for him tonight I'll tell you that Mrs Murphy.'

Another police man hearing her previous answer asked her, 'Do you leave the kids in on their own a lot then Mrs Murphy?'

'No!'

After that another police man who knew my mother came in and started to question her.

'I've told you the kids did it. I battered the little bastards for it.'

'The kids couldn't do that Maria. What's wrong with you? She's your child, why are you protecting him? Are you afraid of Paddy Maria?' But she wouldn't be caught out this time. She stuck to the lie that dad didn't live with her.

'Look Maria, he's a very violent man. If he's doing this to your kid, he's sick. Tell us where he is and let's help him.'

'What's wrong with you lot? My Paddy wouldn't do that. Tell them Sally, please.'

'Our Dad didn't do it, I was telling lies,' I said quietly. They tried but I wouldn't change my story, so eventually they took us home. We went into the house slowly followed by the police, but dad was long gone. After searching the house, the police informed Mum that she'd been reported to the Social Services and that they'd be round in the morning. I felt sick to my stomach that they hadn't caught Dad, and I was knew I was seriously in for it. Mum was really furious with me and shouted at me before we went to bed, 'You swore your father's life away tonight, Sally. I don't like that. No matter what he's your father and you should have never done that.'

Now isn't that great? I thought. He is allowed to almost beat her daughter to death and when I have the guts to report him, which is more than she has the courage to do, she's mad at me. Wow what a mother. I couldn't believe what I was hearing.

'What about how he beats me, Mum?'
'   It's the drink Sally. He loves you really. He does it to me. He doesn't mean it.' I thought about the other stuff that he did to me. I knew that I couldn't tell the police that. I was too ashamed, but I desperately wanted to tell Mum.

'What about what else he does?' I managed, trembling.

'What else?'

But the words wouldn't come, and she wouldn't believe me anyway, 'Oh nothing Mum.'

'The police won't get him Sally, he's been watching them all the while,' Mum told me. I began to shake as this information sank in. However, the police had warned if I had one more mark on my body tomorrow there would be serious trouble.

'Where from Mum?'

'From the house across the road.'

I nearly died of fright. I began to shake as I went up the stairs to bed. What little respect I had for Mum had gone that night. She thought that she was so clever. If Dad hadn't done anything to me, then why did he hide? Why not face the police and defend himself? Suddenly it came to me - he was terrified I had told them that he was sexually abusing me. That was the truth of the matter.

Lying in bed I thought about it, my mind rolling over and over, chasing sleep away. Thought after thought kept me from sleeping. He has never hidden before when I ran away. That went over and over in my mind until eventually exhaustion took over and I drifted off to sleep.

Thankfully my father did not return home that night. In fact, as time drifted by it seemed that he might not return at all. But early the next morning, Mum had a great deal of explaining to do to the social workers who were stood on our doorstep bright and early.

She sat down and started looking at the marks on me and asking questions. Mum stuck to her story and then she asked me. Well, I didn't trust this woman as far as I could throw her. After all, she'd let me down before. She never did anything but ask questions. She'd only leave me here if I did tell which would just seal my death sentence, so I agreed with Mum. She got up to leave knowing she was powerless to prove anything if I refused to talk. But being back at home and knowing Dad was just across the road, how could I?

Weeks went by with no sign of Dad. *He must be really frightened this time*, I thought.

Mum went out a lot. I knew she was meeting him. As the days passed, my nerves began to settle down a bit, but I knew he would eventually return, and he had a long memory. A man and lady started visiting the house and I found out they were more folk from the Social Services.

One night I'd gone to sleep wondering what was happening because I hadn't seen my father in weeks. I woke in the middle of the night to find my father sitting on the end of my bed staring at me. I nearly died of fright. But to my surprise, he lifted me out of the bed and sat me on his lap wrapped his arms around me and hugged me.

I was shitting myself. Tears rolled down his cheeks as he said, 'Forgive me Sally please forgive me. I don't want to hurt you kid, I love you. I can't help it, Sally. Don't always hate me, promise you won't always hate your dad.'

I couldn't relax in his arms, and I wanted him to put me down. I looked at him and I knew he would hurt me again one day. All that kept going through my mind was the filthy things that he had done to me. My disgust must have shown because he started to sob, 'Don't look at me like that Sally, please. You'll understand one day that your dad's sick. Don't hate me, try not to always hate me kid. Say you don't hate me please; do you hate me?'

He was asking me for a love that I no longer knew that I was capable of. Out of fear I replied, 'I don't hate you.'

He held me close, crying like that for what seemed like hours, giving me the creeps. Every bone in my body was on edge waiting for the moment when the monster would return. I felt so sick. My mind played the dirty incidents over and over and I hated him and more than that now, I just wanted him to die. Mum came into the room and put her arms around us. But now I felt pure disgust for her too.

'It's alright Paddy, Sally doesn't hate you. She understands it's the drink.'

I looked at her big belly and wondered how she could let him do that to her. *He's never going to do that to me again,* I swore. *He's not going to give me a baby.* Mum's voice telling him to go broke into my thoughts.

'I don't care let them get me. I deserve it for what I've done to this kid. I've been walking tonight just thinking. I had a real good think about Sally. Her life's hell, I'm wicked to her. You've got to stop me Maria, but you won't, you must stop me. If I kill her, I'll kill you for not stopping me. I love you but you're as bad as me letting me get away with this. You should lock me up, you shouldn't let me do that, she's our first born,' he cried pitifully. 'She's the only one with any guts here Maria. She runs and tells on me; she's got spunk and guts.' He placed me into bed and gently stroked my head before getting into bed with my mother. They started kissing and doing things. The noises they were making turned my stomach.

'I love you, Paddy.'

'I love you, Maria.'

Love my arse I thought. *If that was love, I wanted no part of* it.

CHAPTER 25

A few days later the Social Worker visited my mother. On this visit it was decided that the children should go into care whilst Mum had her ninth child. So, a few days later, the Social Worker returned and took us into care. We went to various homes across the West Midlands.

I loved the fact that I was in a children's home, and only hoped that I might stay forever. It really didn't matter what the place was like, it had to be better than what we had ever known. I had seen all that I ever wanted to of my Father and not to be wicked of course, I prayed to God that something would happen or go wrong so that we would have to stay in care.

My sister and I were taken to a large Children's Home called Erdington Cottage Homes. On entering the gates, we saw lovely lawns with bright flowers surrounding the little gardens in front of many small cottages. There must have been at least seventeen, spread around the grounds, and all of them had the name of fruit, such as Apple Tree, which was the name of the cottage where we were sent to stay.

Entering the house, we were greeted, by a young lady and a man.

'Here we are now girls,' said the Matron as she introduced us to our new home. The house parents and Matron left us standing in the hall for a moment while they went into the office for a chat. I was quite relieved when the house parents came back out of the office.

'Well girls I'm going now so be good,' said the Matron, patting us on the head before leaving. The House Mother then took us into a bathroom where there were three baths, and a young black girl was taking a bath singing away merrily to herself as she did so.

After taking our baths we were then deloused. As always, this took a little time because we were so dirty. Then we went downstairs where we had a lovely big tea and after that the House Mother took us to see where we would be sleeping. It was a large dormitory with about eight beds in it. We gasped at the lovely clean room and homely, pretty way that it was set out, with teddies and dolls on each bed.

We spent three heavenly weeks full of fun, being well cared for and suffering no beatings or fear which was wonderful for me, before the day came that I had dreaded all along. We were playing on the swings when we were called in and greeted by the Childcare Officer who told us to get ready as we would be going home shortly. My sister rushed to get ready, chatting away, full of excitement dying to get home, but I listened silently and took a little longer to get ready, full of disappointment.

I had pushed this day out of my mind so often throughout the past three happy weeks; just thinking about it had made me uneasy. As we left this wonderful place that day, my heart sank, and it took all my strength to fight back the tears. I listened to my sister chat away merrily in the car, but I never spoke a word on the drive home.

Nearing our house, I asked the Childcare officer to stop at the shop so that I could buy my mother and the baby a present with the pocket money I had saved from the home. I bought her a box of chocolates and the baby a rattle.

My Mother greeted us on the door upon our arrival and in her arms, she held the new baby girl. She was a lovely, big, bouncy girl with the loveliest big brown eyes I had ever seen. I loved our new baby and spent many hours changing and feeding her whilst my parents were out. Before the end of our first day home, I was running about making bottles, changing nappies, and nursing the baby, which I quite enjoyed actually.

One afternoon I decided to bath my little baby sister in the bowl and after doing so I dressed her in the clean clothes I laid out on the chair. I made sure to do all of this in front of the fire so she would keep warm. After giving her a bottle, I sat waiting for my parents to come home. But they didn't return that day or night.

It was two days later that they finally showed up. It was nerve racking staying in the house alone at night, so we all went to bed in the attic cuddling together for warmth and comfort, telling each other horror stories, and frightening ourselves to death. Then we couldn't sleep for hours because we were so afraid thinking someone might break in and kill us.

To add to it, I had to go downstairs alone in the pitch blackness to make my baby sister a bottle. I was petrified as I slowly crept down the stairs. I suddenly stepped on a step that creaked and immediately I'd turn and ran back up to the attic shitting myself. I'd stand behind the attic door looking at my siblings sleeping and my baby sister crying for a bottle. My heart was pounding and sweat ran down my forehead as I ran to the baby to cuddle her before I made a gallant attempt to go down and make the bottle again. The baby was hungry and couldn't be consoled which woke one of my younger sisters up her saying, 'Shut that f***ing baby up she's waking me up.'

'Don't be so rotten,' I replied. 'You will have to help me. Now cuddle the baby while I get her bottle.' I remembered that Sally the boxer dog was downstairs and as if she knew I was afraid she came halfway up the stairs to greet me.

My parents returned the next day and the baby had caught a bit of a cold in the night. Dad was slobbering over his new arrival when she sneezed. He called me forward to explain this, 'You aren't looking after my babe right, are ya Scab?'

'I have Dad, I really have!'
I wasn't shocked - this was my life, give all expect nothing but there was no need for this. After all it wasn't my responsibility to take care of the baby, it was theirs. I couldn't understand why they did not seem to realize this.

'I have Dad, I really have!' he mocked pulling me by the hair into the kitchen. 'Now Scab, you have two seconds to speak the truth. How come my child's got a cold?'

'I don't know Dad.'

Of course, I was afraid of my life to tell the truth and say I bathed her. Then my sister innocently piped up, 'Sally looked after her good Dad - she even bathed her for Mum.'

'Why didn't you say you bathed her Scab?'

'I was scared Dad,' I said trembling.

'I'll give you something to be scared about Scab,' he shouted as he dragged me by the hair and threw me across the kitchen table. He hung me upside down on the kitchen door pulled off his leather belt before belting me within an inch of my life. I can still recall the pain as the leather belt lashed off my back sending horrific stinging and burning pains to my flesh and through my system.
    'Now repeat after me Scab. I am a killer. I tried to kill my baby sister. I admit I bathed her so that she would get a cold and die because I am jealous of her.' Wanting this to stop I made a false confession and publicly stated that I was trying to hurt my baby sister.

'She wasn't Daddy, she got up in the night to even feed her,' said one of my sisters.

'Yeah, tried to choke her with her milk you mean!' he replied.

He then told me I had better pray harder than before that my sister did not get worse and die with pneumonia or I would surely die with her. For heaven's sake she only had a sniffle.

For days after that my back ached and stung as I moved my arms and body trying to clean the house but there was no chance of pity seeking in our house. Just one sign of self-pity or sympathy seeking from me was all he was waiting for. He would have gone into a frenzy. So, I had to be strong and struggle on the best I could. Thankfully the baby was fine but that didn't stop him.

Another night he returned home and called me up to the attic. He pulled out his machete knife and had me stand to attention like a soldier while he swung the knife manically in a drunken rage, just past my head, missing by an inch. I trembled but again this was another regular punishment for me.

Oh, he loved mocking me with this one, 'Where's your God now Scab? If he's with you, you'll survive this. If he isn't, then you won't.' The fear of this was just too much for any child never mind me, and I almost crapped myself. This became a regular punishment and one that I most dreaded. So many times, I thought that I was about to meet my end as the knife swung closer and closer to my face and head. I reasoned that if I did survive this, then God must surely be with me, but for the life of me I couldn't understand why he would allow me to suffer like this.

At times like this I questioned my Lord and wondered why my friend Jesus had abandoned me. I prayed silently as I felt the swift coolness of air pass my face as the blade swept past my head. Perspiration flowed freely from my forehead leaving my heart pounding at almost twice its usual pace.

It seemed to go on for hours, stopping each time the knife reached my head to make me stand to attention before starting again. The inner suffering and mental anguish of this torture was indescribable. Every few days, I now had to be subjected to this and for me a little ten-year-old girl, it felt like I was standing before my executioner waiting to be beheaded.

My faith brought me little comfort in this awful inhumane period of my life. Whatever corner I looked for a loving God I could only find a hateful devil. Then I discovered the cross.

One time Mum sent me to the pub on the corner to fetch her usual two large bottles of stout, which was Irish Guinness. It was winter the night was dark and cold, and I waited outside the door for somebody to pass so I could ask them to go into the pub and get me Mum's beer. I was there for ages shuffling and jumping about as kids do to keep warm. I had a shabby jumper on and a summer skirt which was two sizes too big, so it was pinned at my waist with a safety pin.

I looked at all the wet roof tops as they glistened in the light of the moon. I could see the smoke from the chimneys as it rose to the sky into nowhere. I was a compulsive day dreamer and I remember thinking how I wished I was up in the sky so that I could see the whole world and my father could not get hold of me or ever beat me again. As I continued to wait in the dark, spooky, damp corner outside the pub, I glared at the sky and began to quietly pray to Jesus hoping that this time he might hear me.

Suddenly my thoughts were interrupted by my two younger sisters who Mum had sent to see what was holding me up. This task was a job and a half, hanging about outside a pub waiting for an adult to go in so I could ask him to get Mum's booze. Sometimes they said no or even ignored us, which was the correct thing to do. I would imagine they were disgusted that children so young were fetching their parents' beer and hanging around in the dark nights outside a pub, after all, anything could have a happened to us.

I looked up into the sky, and there it was my beautiful blue cross which seemed to be glowing from the sky just for me, saying, 'It's okay Sally. I will never leave you or forsake you.' I walked forward and squeezed my eyes shut to be sure that I was not dreaming but when I opened them it was still there.

I remember thinking, *I wonder if I come back in 20 years will it still be there and what will my life be like?* I let my mind drift as I revelled in the peace of that beautiful blue cross that shone brilliantly through the dark sky. I felt such an overpowering peace looking at that cross and in times to come it was the only thing I could cry to, which seemed to give me hope strength and the courage to persevere onwards through my destructive sordid life.

CHAPTER 26

It got to the stage where my father did not back off me for a minute when he was at home. He was a drunken beast morning, noon and night and I can only describe the things he did to me as the acts of a sick man with a psychopathic nature.

Every time he came in the door, it was me that he wanted. There was no remorse now and never a kind word; he had no compassion not even a glimpse of mercy. He was at me, on me and all over me from dawn to dusk, from the moment he entered the house until the moment he left. He was so paranoid and was determined that I was on a mission to harm, destroy and kill him and his family.

Mother would wash the chipped cups, cracked plates and pots in soap because she couldn't afford washing up liquid, so often when she cooked an Irish stew it tasted soapy. It never occurred to them that washing the utensils in soap might make our food taste soapy. No that was too simple, Dad said that I was putting soap in the stew. Even though I firmly denied doing so, under severe punishment I was forced to say that I did put the soap in the food.

Often, I had to touch a place at the back of our old TV where I would get a nasty shock to which he Mum and some of the siblings' thought was hilarious. For them yes, but torture for me. At other times he would put the poker on the fire until it glowed red and put it as close to my face and hands as he could safely get it without burning me and tell me that if I didn't tell the truth on this matter, I would be getting branded on my face or have to hold the red burning poker in the palm of my hand.

Another little party trick was to lay me on the ground while he sat on my tiny body, put his hands over my nose and mouth and press until I couldn't breathe. While this was happening, my siblings would run around the room and he would call Mum saying, 'Quick Maria look at this. Watch the eyes. I know when to stop.'

That happened quite a lot now and was horrifying. Each time I wondered was this it. Mum just laughed with him as though she was sure he was messing about, and I'd be fine. I often wondered had she forgotten how she felt when he hurt her, but I had never seen him do these sorts of dreadful things to her. Either she had gone mad with him, or she was terrified to stop him.

There was also the cruelty of putting me under the floorboards. Sometimes he would bend me backwards over the fire guard saying as he looked at the clock with his hands around my throat attempting to strangle me, 'On this very day at this very time I could become a murderer.'

I was not allowed to eat with his children and on many occasions, I was made to eat under the table and share the scraps with the dog. With this sort of interrogation, I willingly admitted I had done something I didn't do. But once the interrogation was over and the confession was there it was time for the punishment. It was always bad because Dad couldn't stand a liar and it appeared I was now a liar as well. For putting the soap in the stew, I had to stand by his chair and eat soap. On my life it was so hard to eat some, it tasted so vile.

One of the most horrific memories I have of that time was one day when I was minding the children as usual for my parents while they were out. There was hardly any food in the house and no coal for heating. As the night wore on we were freezing and the little ones began to cry through being cold as they ran about barefooted with just dirty, torn jumpers on.

I knew I couldn't put them to bed for warmth just yet as the beds were more than damp with stale wee and hard in parts with days old muck my mother had not bothered to clean. I knew that they would have only cried themselves to sleep with the cold. Although the filthy bed bothered me a lot, I guess it was warm to them and they had always known this, but I couldn't get used to it. For me it was appalling, and I simply couldn't get into bed to lie in stale piss and lay my face on hard shit until I was too tired to stand. I would dread to think how we smelt to other people in these days.

As the hours passed, the cold in the living room became a little too much for us to handle, so I went to the coal house to see if could find just a little coal or maybe a bucket of slack to build a little fire which would give us some warmth before I put the children to bed. No such luck. There was nothing as Mum had already used the last of it before leaving.

What shall I do? I thought, as I looked at the kids huddled together on the settee. Then I noticed a part of the lino that Mum had already ripped in the corner to burn for heating when times were hard. So, I kept ripping it and burning it until us lot were all happy and warm. I continued to pile the lino on the fire and our spirits rose as we all sat around the grate soaking in the heat. I told them little stories whilst cuddling the twins on my lap, warming their little feet while my sister broke up a few wooden boxes she had found out the back. Not too long after, the babies fell asleep, so I put them to bed.

That night a fight broke out between my two sisters and while I was playing referee trying to stop them, I took a step backwards and somehow fell back too close to the fire setting my dress alight. Luckily, my quick-thinking sister managed to put it out, but I was left with no dress at the back. My main problem was that I didn't have another clean one to get into.

Fear started to rise as I realised that I needed to come up with a good lie to tell my dad about what had happened to my dress. No such gratitude that my life was spared, and I and the children were not burnt ashes as the house burnt to the ground. So, taking a deep breath of relief that we had coped so well in that crisis, I also trembled as panic clawed at my guts. I knew what fate lay ahead of me shortly and it seemed better to jump in the fire now and be done with it once and for all, but I hadn't the guts.

I could just imagine the rotten nasty child abuser sitting in the pub with his pint getting slowly drunk, bragging about what a great husband and father he was, all the while planning my torture for the night.

When they eventually did roll in, Dad decided he was going to teach me never to play with fire again. So, he stamped on some more thin market boxes which we're piled in the yard, broke the wood up and slung it on and began to stoke up the fire. Now get this one, to stop me from hurting my siblings and burning myself in the future, I was dragged to the fire grate pleading for mercy and screaming in panic where he forced my right hand and for a few second held it in the flames of the blazing fire. I struggled desperately to get it out. The pain was unspeakable but I was no match for him and so he burnt me.

I gasped with pain as the skin popped on my burning flesh. Stabbing pains began to shoot up my whole arm and a layer of skin was burnt off my hand. When he let me go, I crawled to the corner of the room whining like a little wounded animal as I nursed my right hand. It was blistered with raw flesh hanging out in places and it throbbed and wept. The pain was unbearable.   A strange look of compassion suddenly crossed his face, 'Sorry kid, I didn't mean to hurt you so much. But I had to do it to stop you playing with fire; otherwise, you might burn yourself to death.'

Bloody heck, imagine what he would do if I played in the road, sling me under a bus? He told Mum to hold it under the tap and wrap a piece of rag around it. Mum told him she thought I needed to go to hospital as it looked really bad.

'Na she'll be fine,' he said. 'Now put her to bed.'

There was no room in the kid's bed that night, so dad laid me in the baby's cot beside their bed.

'That's bad,' he said lifting my hand. 'I didn't mean to hurt you this badly. Does it pain?'

'Yes Dad, it's killing me,' I sobbed.

It must have been too much for him to take because he stormed off upstairs and made my Mum cover my hand. I'll never forget the look of horror and disgust on her face as she held my hand in hers. I couldn't help but think *she thinks he's gone too far this time*. What my mother did not realize was that he had gone too far from the moment he had begun to abuse me.

'The dirty f***ing bastard, there's no need for that. I'll get him for this Sally,' she said with tears streaming down her face. 'This is too much now. He's going to end up killing you if I don't put a stop to this and get this bastard lifted for it! I'll sort that swine before the night's out Sally.'

'Oh no Mum please don't start on him,' I sobbed. 'He'll only start on me again.'

Eventually they came up to bed and I pretended to be sleeping in the cot as they fornicated beside me. The sound of that always disturbed me and I found it so hard to sleep with the pain of my burn. You would have thought they might have even thought about getting me a pain killer but no.

I could do little for a few days as I had a huge weeping blister that went across the front of my right hand. Even Dad knew at this point that I needed hospital treatment.

As time passed, he continued to sexually violate me, sometimes in the very room where the children played, and they didn't notice. It's amazing what can go on in a room unnoticed. They got an old piano from somewhere; I don't know why for I don't think anyone could play. The kids banged away making a right racket at times but that was about it.

Mum went out this one evening leaving him to mind us. She was off to scrounge some cash of his brother. It seemed I had played up, so I had to stand on top of the piano on one leg for a while and the children and Dad thought it was hilarious. I wasn't the best at balancing, and I had a fear of heights, so their amusement added to my distress.

Later that evening he put a towel over his lap opened his trousers and put my head under the towel forcing me to put my face where I hated it being. It didn't leave much to the imagination what I was being forced to do. Now and again one of the children passed stood looked and asked Dad, 'What's Sally doing there?'

'Oh, she's being punished,' he replied.

Mum came back with the cash and after feeding us a sausage sandwiches and custard cream biscuits they went off to the pub. As always, I could hear Dad's steel cap shoes on their return from the pub. Mum sang away in the street at the top of her voice and Dad tried to shut her up. This is where I shook knowing I was minutes away from whatever was to come.

This night they fought themselves and he battered her as she slung things at him, but she wasn't in the mood to give in. I hid under the bed with my younger siblings, and we all hugged together defenceless and terrified. It was an utterly pitiful sight which we did not deserve or want. If only they knew how their fighting and drinking affected their children, would they have stopped? No, I fear not for they were alcoholics, who were self-centred and selfish to the core. All they could think about was themselves, not even each other, just 'self'. And being so self-absorbed, nothing else seemed to matter outside of that. For it was, and always had been, all about them.

The fight made its way up the stairs and Dad knocked her onto the bed bursting her lip. He went downstairs to sleep on the settee, but she was in no mood to surrender this night and suddenly my mother stormed out of the bedroom and grabbed the piss and shit bucket on the stairs. She went down to where he was lying and slung the contents of the bucket all over my father, before hitting him over the head with a bottle. That night ended up with them fighting in the street and Dad being arrested. He was sentenced to a month in prison which suited me fine.

CHAPTER 27

Whilst my father was in prison the Social Worker asked Mum if she would give her permission for me to go into an open-air school in the country. My Mother said she couldn't do this because my father would go crazy. So, the Social Worker said she'd visit him in prison and ask him herself. To my surprise, he said yes. I never really understood that and could not help but wonder what made him agree to let me go. Maybe he had an unusual moment of compassion, or maybe guilt just got the better of him.

Before this dad had asked Mum to go and get a photo taken of her and all the children. So, she took us all around to the photography studio where the photographer was to take a photo of her and the children. Suddenly Mum said, 'No not you Sally. Maybe next time. It's just me and the kids on this photo.'

Even the photographer was surprised at this and asked, 'Is Sally not your little girl?'

'Yes', she answered abruptly.

I believe that when she took the photo up to my father a few days later, he asked her where I was and told her that I should be on it. She went to visit him almost daily and always took a few of the children - or all of them except me. Never once did she think to ask me to go with them, so I stayed at home and cleaned the house.

Again, I believe he said to her one day, 'Maria why haven't you brought Sally to visit me again? She's my daughter too and you haven't taken her photo and never bring her to visit, it's not right, please bring her up to see me.'

'Paddy, I thought you couldn't stand her. I didn't want to annoy or upset you!'

'You're upsetting me not bringing her Marie. Can you imagine how she feels?'

Well, I never, him actually caring how I feel! But come to think of it he was off the drink again. Come to think of it, the few times I had witnessed him sober, he actually seemed the better and most caring parent.

Whatever the reason for not taking me mattered little now, for a few days later the Social Worker returned to take me to what was to be my new home for a while. Because I had no coat and no decent clothing, she kindly brought me some. The coat was red and three sizes too big for me. Mum loved it and it would have fitted her, but she could hardly ask me for it in front of the Social Worker. It came to my ankles but nevertheless I was grateful for it.

We said our goodbyes and Mum stood crying at the door as the Social Worker drove off with me. I am unsure what that was about for I couldn't see how it was love. More like she had lost her housekeeper, come children's nanny, come cook, come general dogs' body and all out skivvy.

We drove through the city and went on till we got to some long country lanes. I chatted away excitedly loving every minute of it. The school driveway was so long. It was a massive place were hundreds of girls lived, aged between five and sixteen.

The Head Mistress greeted us. She was a very stern and smart Scottish woman in her late forties I would say, and I liked her welcome.

The Social Worker left after a little chat with the Head in private and as it was dinner time, I was taken into the dining room by the head teacher to meet the girls. I gasped with surprise seeing so many girls as they all looked at us silently in respect of the head mistress entering the room.

'This is Sarah. I want you to be nice to her and look after her. Do you hear girls?'

'Yes Miss,' they all replied as one.

My eyes were drawn to a group of girls about my age who were sitting on a table close by. They were huddled together, whispering and giggling. I wondered what they could be laughing at then it dawned on me – it was me. I looked a right state.

I was small for my years and very thin with a very pale complexion and tatty hair. My small frame was smothered in my big red coat which revealed only a part of my shabby grey socks, callipers, and almost worn-out cripple boots beneath. I hated to be laughed at, it humiliated me, and I became furious as I went red with embarrassment and shouted with anger, 'Who you f***** laughing at?'

The whole room went into a shocked silence and the head mistress was flabbergasted as I continued to roar in pure rage, 'Don't you dare laugh at me again. I'll batter you if you do, you cheeky bastards!' It took a moment for the head to recover from the shock before she silenced the giggling and laughing girls with one look.

'Now, now Sarah, we do not use that foul language in this school. I want no more of it from now on.' I hung my head in shame as she led me to a table. The stares of the girls almost burned into my back as I sat down at the table. Some girls made the effort to try and talk to me, but I was still feeling quite angry, so I ignored them.

If they think they're going to bully or pick on me, they're in for a right shock, I vowed. Being so scruffy had not really bothered me before. I was used to it and did not look out of place at home, for nearly everybody was scruffy where I lived. But these girls were clean and by the way they spoke it was obvious that they came from pretty good homes. It was a school for those with health problems and that's what they were here for, eczema and asthma and things like that. I started to think about my bad leg as there did not seem to be anybody else in here who was handicapped.

I looked around deep in thought. Suddenly I noticed a girl of about sixteen with a hump on her back carrying a tray full of fresh cream doughnuts around. I did not like it too much as the girls on my table started laughing at her and calling her 'Humpy'. She stopped at our table.

'Hello Sarah, my name's Christine. If you come find me after dinner, I'll show you around. Would you like that?'

'Yes thanks.'

She carried on to the next table and the girls around me resumed their giggling and whispering behind her back. I did not like that at all and once more I did not like being in this school with these snobs. Oh, they were having a right good laugh about her and one of them turned to me and said, 'I bet you're damned glad you haven't got a hump like her aren't you, Sarah?' That was all I needed to get me angry as I flared at them in temper, 'You cheeky two faced horrible, spoiled bastards.'

I bet they'll be calling me names next. Yeah, well I'll give them something to think about, I thought before continuing to say, 'You'll get a hump on your face in a minute if you carry on bothering me you snobs!'

'Oh? Do you think that you're capable enough then? Well, we'll see about that after dinner now won't we,' she replied in her posh voice,

'Yeah, we will,' I answered. Another one said if I continued to be rude and disagreeable, she would report me to the head, and I was sure to receive a jolly good spanking with the slipper in assembly the next morning.

'Tell them I don't give a shit and I'm telling ya now, no one is going to fucking slipper me!'

I don't think these girls had been in the company of a person such as I before. I don't think they believed people such as I existed. We were worlds apart. It must have looked like I had fallen right out of a Dickens novel to them.

She then went to get some more tea and one of the other girls on our table whispered to me, 'You should watch what you're saying to her Sarah, she's the cock of our year and she is sure to bash you.'

'Is she? Well, she won't be for long if she starts on me, I'm telling you,' I replied. One of the things the years of abuse had given me was a fighting spirit.

After dinner I was taken to the nurse who cleaned my head, bathed me, and creamed my eczema. Then I was taken to the laundry where I put my clothes and dressed in only a dressing gown I was then taken to the linen room and given a nice new school uniform. There was a nice pair of pants and a vest. A green pleated skirt, white shirt and green jumper, a pair of long green socks for me because of my calliper and boots and a white hanky all with number thirty-five on, which was to be my number. I felt very smart in my uniform and loved wearing it even though the other girls hated theirs.

Christine met me and showed me around the school. We chatted for a while, and she told me a lot about herself. I told her all about my lovely brothers and sisters and we talked about records, TV, and dancing. It turned out we had a great deal in common. She was a really nice girl and promised to come and see me again after school as she took me to my class.

The bully was in the classroom sitting on the back desk like Lady Muck with all the girls gathered around her. She gave me a dirty look and put her nose in the air, demanding attention as she yapped away about boys that fancied her. The teacher came in and the afternoon lessons passed quite quickly. At four o'clock, the bell signalled the end of class, and the teacher gathered her books and left the room. I looked back at the girl and knew by the expression on her face that she was ready to fight. There was no way I was going to chicken out of this. She needed teaching a lesson.

As I got up, she said, 'Where are you going Hoppy Leg?' The girls around her tittered and laughed at this.

'Nowhere if you want me,' I replied calmly. They bombarded me with insults and taunts which only inflamed me more.

'Can't your mother afford some decent clothes for you then?'

'She's got nits as well.'

'Pooh, smell the stuff in her hair. What a Flea-bitten bitch.'

'Was that your mother's coat you borrowed?'

Endless insults were slung at me by several different girls thinking they were so clever in their bully like fashion. At that all the girls started to laugh as they slowly gathered around me, poking me, and pulling the ends of my hair with the tips of their fingers. I became furious and knew this was a case of kill or be killed and they scattered back as I swung into a bunny punch. As the ringleader came forward, I smacked her right in her face. Either she was slow, or I was very fast because before she could move, I was on her whilst she lay on the floor, pulling her hair.

It was like I had opened Pandora's Box. Every emotion that I had bottled up inside, all the rage, humiliation, hurt and resentment that I had hidden inside and suffered at the hands of my Father, was released in that moment. I booted and punched her, ignoring her screams. I was blind with rage and the next thing I remember was hearing a teacher's voice telling me to stop.

I looked down at the girl on the floor. She was in a poor state. Her hair was all over the place. Her eye was swollen, and her lip was burst. I heard the voice telling me to stop and saying that they didn't tolerate such behaviour in that school but all I could think was that she deserved it.

As the weeks drifted by, I felt uncomfortable and did not like the school at all. I just did not seem to fit in. I was very aggressive, so the girls made sure to be my friend and leave me alone, but I didn't speak a lot. I was just polite or snotty if I felt a bit down. I tried to be polite to the teachers, but I always seemed to say something wrong, and they would show me up making me repeat it until I withdrew into myself and became very stubborn.

Don't get me wrong, compared to home I loved it but by now I was a very emotionally damaged little girl and needed far more support and even child counselling than we were getting here. The nurse did not seem to like me at all, and it was never more evident than the day I started my periods.

I remember visiting the toilet after breakfast and noticing what had happened, I went along to the surgery to see her. It was crowded so I hung back full of embarrassment, trying to build up the courage to try and tell her. There were three older girls left in the room when she spotted me, 'What are you hanging around for Sarah? What do you want?'

'I'd like to speak to you alone please nurse.'

'Don't be so silly Sarah, come on, out with it. What's wrong?'

'There's blood on my pants Nurse.' She then proceeded to pull my pants down in front of these three girls and gave me a demonstration of how to use a sanitary towel. I could have died on the spot.

Another thing that bothered me was there was a big boy's school over the road, and we had to go to Mass with them on a Sunday. I did not like that at all as they gave me the nickname of Peg Leg. That really did hurt my feelings, and I would go back into the school and just get even madder. I hated my leg. It wasn't my fault that I had it so couldn't understand why they made me feel so different. I asked the teacher could I stay at school on Sundays, but she said no, so I asked her could I wear trousers, but she just told me not to be so silly.

It was then discovered that I needed glasses and to top it all off I was made to wear my National Health round John Lennon specks for church which was not the fashion item of the day and screamed out we were on the social security, so you can imagine the mocking I got from some of the boys. This was also hammering away at my already low-self-esteem.

After a month I went home on our school holidays and to my relief Dad was still in prison. It was during this time that I had my first ever kiss with a boy. It was with the boy across the street and just for a few moments, I allowed myself to be a girl. I suppose I fancied him deep at heart and really did want him to kiss me, but I was scared, and I didn't know why. I was just afraid of this physical contact from a boy.

He was a year older than me, 13 and very tall. He was good looking and a great scrapper, but he was also very quiet and gentle with it and only fought when he had to. Suddenly he grabbed me and kissed me right on the lips. My initial reaction was panic but there was something different about his intentions that made me relax. I got a tingle and butterflies in my tummy which I could not understand.

All too soon I went in the house and made some tea floating on air, in love and in a world of my own. After some time, I drifted off to sleep full of pleasant girlish thoughts of the boy across the road who gave me my first ever real kiss. A few days later I went back to the school.

CHAPTER 28

I soon settled back into my open-air school which was in the most beautiful part of the countryside and began to love this normal way of living. There were a couple more school holidays after that first one. I was greeted by my father on the last and he seemed so pleased to see me. He chatted away about the school and hugged me and told me to sit on his knee and give him a cuddle. For me it was a huge discomfort and put me at ill ease.

I was sprouting boobies and had started my monthlies and there was no way I was going to allow him to ever touch me like that again. By now I realized the full impact of his attraction to little girls, and I could only hope and pray he wasn't getting at my little sisters.

Mum didn't like me sitting on his knee and ordered me off saying I was far too old to be sitting on my father's lap. With him as a Father I utterly agreed but good decent Dads could sit their children on the knees forever if they wanted. I was glad she took me off his knee, it bothered Dad more than it did me. Through-out my visit home Dad didn't hurt me in anyway at all. He kept his hands to his self and his penis in his pants, and all too soon I was back off to school.

I was thirteen now and really thriving at this school. I had put weight on; my hair was glossy and looked thicker. I was well dressed and well-polished and becoming well-spoken again. We had so many activities at school. I was a girl guide and went camping in the school grounds. There was a huge swimming pool in the grounds too, so once a week we went swimming in the summer. We had barn dances with the boys over in the boy's school very Tuesday evening. I loved dancing and we had dance nights at our own school each week too. I was so at home there and had begun loving my life.

One Saturday night I was restless, and a teacher woke me to tell me to get up and have a wash and change myself while she changed my bed. It seemed I had vomited in my sleep.

'What time is it, Miss?' I asked half-awake and ready to trot off and wash as she had asked.

'Eleven-forty-five,' she said. It appeared I had chucked-up everywhere in my sleep which was unlike me.

The following Monday I was sitting in class when a knock came to the classroom door. An older girl entered and spoke quietly to my teacher and after she left my teacher called me to her desk.

'Miss Armstrong wants to see you Sarah,' she said straightening my tie, so I looked smart.

'Why does the head want me, Miss? Have I done something wrong?'

'No, you're not in trouble Sarah, now go and knock on Miss Armstrong's office door, there's a good girl!'

So off I went and knocked.

'Come in Dear and sit down,' said the head. 'Sarah, last Saturday night there was a fight at your home. There's no easy way to say this to you. Your Father was stabbed and has died dear!' I sat stunned, unable to comprehend what I had just heard. I'd been called to the headmistress' office minutes earlier expecting to be told off for fighting again or something, but never this. How could it be true?

I heard myself saying, 'You mean he's dead Miss?'
'Yes Sarah,' she said quietly.

'Is my Mum alright?'

'Yes, Sarah she is being looked after.'

'What about my brother and sisters?' I said beginning to get quite anxious and upset now.

'Everybody at your home is being supported dear.'

'Do you know what time this happened to Dad Miss?'

She cleared her throat, 'I heard it was after the pub.'

'What happened Miss?' I said desperate for answers.

She shifted in her seat, 'I believe that there was a fight in your home and your father was killed. He did not live with you anyway now did he dear, so you would not have really known him that well?'

How wrong she was. Mum always said he did not live with us because she was claiming the national assistance as a single Mother, but not only did he live with us, we truly felt his presence. As awful as I felt this man was, I did not wish such a cruel end to him. My thoughts were interrupted by the Head, 'Sarah are you alright Dear?'

'Yes Miss,' I replied as tears slowly trickled down my face. 'Okay Sarah, you may return to class now,' she said dismissing me. I left the room numb, baffled and deeply worried for my mother and siblings. I didn't know why I was silently sobbing. *Why did this bother me so much*? I couldn't help but wonder. After all, this man had brutalized me and I had every reason to hate him, but never-the-less his death deeply upset me. I didn't know what to think as a million thoughts scrambled through my mind and left me utterly stunned, as I slowly walked down the long staircase. My eyes began streaming with tears when suddenly my legs buckled, and I fell down the stairs. A teacher rushed to me, and I was told to leave class and rest or walk or sit on the grass until I felt a little better.

A week later I was returned home. The house was poor, grimy, and chaotic as usual. The children were boisterous, unkempt, and demanding. They ran to me full of disturbing excited chatter.

'Sal Dad got stabbed,' one shouted.

'There was blood everywhere Sal!' another said.

'It was them Bastards over the road!' another child shouted. They we're all shouting trying to be heard so I couldn't really hear anybody and realizing this one of my younger sisters shouted out, 'Shut the f@** up Bastards and talk one by one!'

She had a way with words my sister, 'Do it now or I'll punch your head in.'

'Look Sal, there's Dads bloody hand mark on the wall he'll haunt us now," said one of my little brothers. I looked to the wall and saw the blood-stained handprint of my Father. My younger brother ran to the blood stain and began to act out Dad's final moments. If it wasn't so sad one could almost burst into laughter.

They began telling me about every detail in their own little vulgar way but to me they were so beautiful and cute. How could they know any different? This was all they knew and saw from the day they we're born. How could they speak any other way for this was all they had heard from the time they could remember! Yet the saddest thing of all was the fact that all this talk and all these behaviours coming from such little one's would have horrified most people but was so normal to the children and me. The older ones began to give me a detailed account of what took place that night of father's murder.

It seems Father had been put in jail again, and he was bailed out of prison that very day and killed by his friend. He had been sober for a few weeks and wanted to settle a little and try to keep out of trouble. He went to see his brothers and sisters to stay. He promised to come and see the kids that night and take Mum out for a drink, but his sister didn't want him to leave that night. She said she had a bad feeling and begged him to stay, but he felt he had to go and see Mum and the kids and so he did.

My Aunt said years later she'd had a strange feeling so slipped a St Christopher's medal in his pocket as he left to protect him. She felt she couldn't give it to him for he would receive nothing he saw as religious or superstitious. So true to his word he visited his kids and took Mum for a drink, then went back to the house to see the kids as he dropped mum off, had a quick cuppa and attempted to leave and go back to his dad's house where a few of his unmarried siblings lived, to give himself time to straighten out his life.

Mum wanted him to stay but he wouldn't, so she walked him to the door and stood watching as he walked off up the street towards the city to catch his bus. Suddenly Shirley from next door, the adulteress, started trouble with Mum accompanied by the woman across the road and Shirley's husband was out there too. Mum screamed as they pulled her to the ground and Dad hearing the commotion looked around to seeing my mother being attacked. He ran back to pull them off her, but Shirley's husband went fist to fist with him. Dad battered him. Then the other one's husband ran over, and Dad battered him too. A couple of passers-by tried to intervene to stop it but to no avail. People went into their houses closed the door and peeped through the curtains.

It all seemed to quieten down, and Dad walked Mum and the kids back home.

'Daddy don't go please!' came the cries from his deeply hysterical children. Just then a huge bang came on the door. The kids froze. It seems Dad looked at Mum and told her to get the children up the stairs, but they were panic stricken and refusing to move, screaming, and shuffling their feet on the spot in sheer bewilderment and panic at what was happening. For seconds they endlessly pleaded fear stricken, 'Don't open the door please Daddy!'

Dad opened the door and in ran the woman from over the road shouting abuse. She launched herself at my father with a knife; she was quickly followed by her husband who began to fight with Dad. The women turned and stabbed dad in the back and the back of the head while the man plunged a knife into father's heart. My sister told me how he staggered back leaving the bloody handprint on the wall and fell to the ground. For some reason it seems the couple then bent down grabbed him and dragged his body out into the road, closely followed by screaming children and my mother who we're all terrorized, traumatized, and stunned with disbelief at this point. In the middle of the road, they stood and knelt alone surrounding the body of my father.

My Mother lost her mind and began to mourn very loudly sending chills up the children's spines. She then began to bathe her face in the blood from his bleeding wounds on his chest. She endlessly mourned, smearing the blood his all over her face, neck, and hair. She then started to smear the blood all over each of his children covering their tiny faces in it. It must have been a sight to behold. Yet not one person came near them to even remove and comfort the screaming, panic stricken little children until the police arrived.

In all that despair Shirley full of anger ran over to my younger sister and hit her straight over the head with a sweeping brush knocking her straight out. So now there lay two bodies in the road, father lay dead and my poor weak battered little sister. My eyes filled with tears as they revealed their story, and I wondered what effect this would have on them being so young.

'Mum said it was quarter to twelve when Dad was pronounced dead,' my sister finished. I was shocked as my thoughts flew back to the Saturday night at the school when I awoke vomiting. I got chills through my spine. It was exactly 11.45. Almost as he took his last breath, I threw out a huge vomit. Spiritually minded people might think that at his departure from this cruel world that something of him left me at that moment.

Chapter 29

It was a cold dreary day when we arrived at the funeral parlour, and I was feeling very spooked. I hated these sorts of places not that I had ever been in one before, but to me they housed death and that gave me the creeps. Dad was in there and that scared me shitless.

All father's brothers and sisters started to arrive and apart from nodding at my mother they proactively ignored us all. My Uncle came over to us standing together and asked which child my father had given his last words too. Mum pointed to my sister; he asked her what he'd said to which she replied, 'Look after your mother and the children.'

He looked at Mother and said, 'She is the only one we want to know.' There stood three girls and two boys in a chilly, frightening funeral home, waiting for them bring out their Father's coffin, all very confused and terribly afraid, and here was Dad's elder brother telling us they were only interested in one of Father's children, not all of them. How awful was that? I could only put it down to their grief! But no such understanding came from Mum, and she hugged her young ones and told my lovely Uncle in no uncertain terms what an ole bollocks he is.

She couldn't resist saying loudly to them, 'They're all his bleeding children you nasty bastard!' Suddenly the coffin was carried out. Dad's brother said, 'Here he comes', and everyone sobbed as they put the coffin into the Hearse. I can't remember the Church service – just all the people wearing black.

The Hearse drove us down to our street and stopped outside our house for a few minutes. The street was empty and silent with an almost eerie morbidness about it. A few curtains moved where people peeped, but there was clearly no love for this family. I could understand them being upset with my parents but surely not the innocent children.

There was a lot happening in that street and I guess many people just didn't know what to do and didn't want to get involved. There was our house, we being the victims, and next door was Dad's ex-lover, the family who instigated the trouble that night, and over the road on the other corner was the other large family whose parents were the murderers. It was rumoured that dad had fornicated with her too – a very strange state of affairs in-deed.

A couple of the younger children who were far too young to attend the funeral were home and one of the younger boys seeing us in the big black Hearse outside the window, ran out straight to the Hearse and slapped the window shouting sadly. He was the little fella Dad adored and he couldn't have been older than three and a half to four. When Dad lay in bed most mornings, he would shout my brother's name and my little brother would shout back, 'Arsehole daddy- Arsehole!' Dad had taught him to say that as it amused the socks off him.

As young as my tiny, sweet brother was it seemed he had a full awareness that Daddy was in that big black car in that big brown box. So, he banged away at the window and almost breaking the hearts of the drivers and all present he shouted, 'Dad, Daddy come on! Come out of there! Come home! It's me your babe! Come here Daddy!'

The babysitter gently picked him up to carry him in as he screamed, 'I want my Daddy! Daddy arsehole Daddy arsehole!' Those pitiful words echoed in my ears. 'I want to go with them, Daddy, Daddy!' he sobbed as she closed the door and we drove off towards the graveyard. That just broke people up on the spot.

The gates of the graveyard look so huge and creepy as we entered. It was a grim day which matched the mood of everyone who stood around his gave weeping. We children stood at the front next to the big hole with the coffin on with Mum. As I stared at the gruesome coffin, I could hear father's voice saying in my thoughts, 'You will never get away from me scab, even if I die you will never get away from me, I will haunt you!' Suddenly a loud cry snapped me back to reality as they lowered coffin into the ground.

I remember covering my face with a hanky because I began to laugh with my nerves, so I had to pretend I was crying. I was emotionally damaged and part of that meant that at times I was emotionally out of control of my feelings. It manifested in ways such as this - I would laugh when I should cry, and I cried when I should laugh. It happened at the most inappropriate times – like my father's funeral. I was all messed up inside and didn't know how to begin to work myself out.

After that things got from bad to worse for Mother and she really couldn't cope with us all. She was drinking very heavily, running around with another guy and never home. She thought nothing of sending myself or my younger sisters to the chemist to get a packet of Durex. It did not take us long to work out what they were for and seeing that dad was now dead we couldn't understand why on earth she would need them.

The reality of it all became very clear to me; she was now picking men up in the pubs of a night and prostituting herself for cash. Sometimes she took us to the pub with her and I would have to stand out-side all night until closing where she always came out with a dirty old man, and we went off with him. Sometimes I had to wait at the end of an entry for her. I guess I could truly understand if she did this to fund the children, but it was for alcohol and to be honest, I found this offensive.

One night after mom got turfed out of the pub at closing time, we were walking towards the bus stop with another dirty old perv. Mum was giggling with him, and I walked slightly ahead disgusted. He tried to say hello to me a couple of times, but I just ignored him saying, 'Come on Mum we have to go.' Again, he said, 'Hello, so Sally's your name what a fine girl you are!'

To which I ignored him again when Mum suddenly said, 'Don't be so fucking ignorant and answer him!'
'I Don't want to talk to him Mum, I don't like him!'

Turning to my mother he said, 'Look at her; she'll make a good one when she's older!'

A good what? I thought, *a good prostitute like you mum.* I gave him the dirtiest look you could imagine as if he was filth on the sole of my shoe. I waited in the cold again as Mum went down a back street. I was the lookout – knowing to duck if I saw a blue light.

Suddenly Mum appeared running down the entry. Grabbing my hand, she told me to run. We were just in time to jump on a bus and as we looked back the old pervert was looking at us on the bus fuming. I was delighted and gave him a huge grin then and the two fingers as I went upstairs on the bus with Mum.

We sat in the back seat and Mum was killing herself laughing. Pulling something out of her pocket she said, 'Got the dirty ole Bastards wallet,' and we both laughed as we made our way home.

At times when we woke up to no food, Mum would tell me to go to the Catholic Priest's house. This was one of the things that I found mortifying, and with great embarrassment I would go to the Priest's home and ask him for money for the electric meter, which we never really had, because she kept breaking into the money meter, and ask him for a bag of food. He always gave it.

We moved house very quickly as they understood why Mother never wanted to stay in the house her husband was murdered in. We went to another inner-city council house, in yet another vile area of Birmingham. Mother began to bring her much younger lover home. He was in-fact handsome and a nice person.

There was eleven months between one of my sisters and I, and although times were hard and we didn't have much to look forward to with our hillbilly lifestyles, as well as tears there very many laughs. I recall Mum's lover stayed over a lot of the time - he really was a good guy and we all liked him. He made Mum happy, so she was pleasant enough and life was easier even though my sister and I still had to do all the chores, cooking, and child minding.

This one morning I was sitting in the impoverished living room and my sister was making a cuppa for a change in the kitchen. Mum's lover came in saying a cheerful, 'good morning, Sal', as he did a hand stand up against the wall. Suddenly as he was upside down his zip was open and I caught a glimpse of his willy. He must have gone to the loo and forgot to zip up or had a broken zip, because he really was a decent person who we felt safe with, so I knew it was accidental.

Anyway, as he stood on his hands up the wall and I saw this, blushing with embarrassment I went into my sister in the kitchen and told her he had done a handstand and I had accidently seen his penis.

'Come on, let's have a look,' said my sister. '

'What?' I replied as she waltzed into the living room with me on her trail, and we sat on the chairs. He was reading a newspaper by now and my sister came out with, 'Do us a hand-stand Tony – go on!'

'I'm reading now bab,' he replied.

'Go on please your brilliant at it Sally said!'

He got up and did one, but nothing happened this time. So, my sister walked off saying, 'It's okay thanks Tony. Sally said your dick fell out!' I almost died.

'Yeah, sorry about that Sal it was my zip giving me problems. I need new jeans I had to pin these up.'

Tony saw the mountain of work I did and would often hear him say to Mum, 'You really need to give that kid a break, Marie. She's a lovely girl and the only one who can't see that is you. She does everything for you, and you have no time for her. You need to stop saying, "Sally's a pretty kid, but you should see my other daughter," in front of her.

'Imagine how she feels when you say that? That doesn't make you look good, people thinking you think one kid is better than another, that's not good Marie.'

Mum didn't like that, but she liked him. I can remember baby-sitting one night, when a social worker knocked on the door. As always, we stayed silent and ignored her knocking, then lifting the letter- box she called to me, 'Come on Sarah we know you're in!'
She wasn't going away that night, so I felt there was something different happening. She went off after about ten minutes, so I told my two younger sisters to run and get Mum from the pub quickly. 'And if the social worker comes back while you're out there, hide until she's gone right girls?' I told them.

'Yes Sal!' they replied obediently before running off to get Mum.

Suddenly the door banged again, and she called, 'Please open up Sarah we know your there, come on dear!' We sat quiet ignoring her as we'd done so many times before. But it's impossible for seven young kids to stay silent and hide.

'Sarah, I know you're there, now come to the door dear. Come on Sarah, open the door there's a good girl!'

Suddenly we jumped as a knock came to the back window. I looked up to see a police man standing at the back window. He knocked on the window glass continuing to stare straight at us as we all hugged together. Then looking directly at me and I eye to eye with him only separated by glass and again he said, 'Come on Sarah please open the door. The games up now - I am looking at you so we know you are in. Now stop being a silly girl and let me in dear!'

'No!' I replied stubbornly. 'I am not allowed to answer the door when Mum isn't here. You must wait. She won't be a minute!' 'So, you agree your Mum's out then Sarah and had left you all alone again?'

Realising my mistake, I quickly answered 'Yes I agree she is out across the yard in the toilet!' I was delaying for time now hoping Mum had the sense to sneak around the back and make it look like she had been the Lavvy. I had told Mum to cover that back-room window - *now what can I do*? I thought.

Again, the policeman began to say, 'Be a good girl and open the door, we have to come in and I don't want to kick the door in!'

He went away but five minutes later he was back with another policeman and the social worker. We thought he wouldn't be back again; they never had before. Then they looked at us through the window and as he knocked again the policeman said, 'Can you open the door please Sarah, we have to come in now dear!'

'Nope, sorry I don't want to be rude but me Mum will be back from the toilet soon!'

'Okay Sarah, we shall wait right here for her,' and they did.

In the next moment Mum flew in the front door with my sisters and it was apparent she was tipsy. This wasn't going to be easy for her to talk her way out of as the police officers and social workers asked her to open the door which she did.

They went right through the house, and it was filthy. Half-dressed, unkempt, raggedy noisy little kids ran about the house manically almost disrupting their house search. They all took lots of notes and sadly for my mother, it was pretty blatant, the magnitude of the neglect that had manifested through this impoverish despicable unhealthy home.

I heard one police officer say to another, 'You wouldn't keep animals in these conditions.'

He became a little embarrassed when he realized I had heard, but I smiled at him to show I was not offended. I *have been running away trying to tell you this for years – now you listen!* I thought. There were no parenting classes in these days and even if there were, and they were free, unless our Mum was getting money for booze to take them, she would have never bothered.

She was given an immediate summons to bring all of us to the child protection court the next morning. She did, having no choice, and all of us were placed into the care system that moment. Now although it was brilliant to be in care for me, I had become very attached to my brothers and sisters, but we were split up and scattered around children's homes in the West Midlands. I mean who was going to house nine children? We had all lost so much in our young lives and yet we had to lose more, in-fact all we had – each other!

CHAPTER 30

My father was just thirty-six years old when he was murdered and as crazy and as cruel as he appeared; I felt that it was a harsh death. A part of me felt he was brave due to the fact he had said his last words to my younger sister. Those words showed he clearly knew he'd had chips and was about to kick the bucket. I remember learning from the Bible when the nuns shoved it down my throat at times that if you live by the sword, you die by it and that certainly seemed to be true for Dad.

Going into care wasn't so bad, I mean anything had to be better that what we had all lived through. In-fact we thrived in care, the only downside was that we were shifted from one care home to another. The good thing was that we got to get visits with each other at times (except for two of my brothers, who were in Father Hudson homes which was in the same grounds as St Gerald's, the hospital where I had stayed for many years and loved so much.)

I spent school holidays in care homes and was back to learning in the residential school throughout school term. Something that really impressed me once was the Head mistress allowing all my little brothers and sisters to come and have tea with me at the school. She must have gone to great lengths to organize this afternoon trip for them, not to say having them all brought out to the countryside from all their very different care homes.

We had such a delightful time as the younger ones ran about the splendid grounds full of excitement. My siblings were spoiled rotten by the teachers and girls, and this became a memory that many of us grew to cherish as the years piled by. These years although pleasant most of the time helping us to feel a bit more secure, were also a very confusing and unsettling time for us, but there was no more violence, or hunger and we never lived in filth or got cold, so I counted my blessings.

But growing up in care wasn't easy either. Regardless to the fact that I was always on the move throughout these utterly insecure, sensitive, adolescent years of my life, it also had its benefits, the biggest one being that I felt safe. In the care system I guess we were seen as challenging children from a troubled history.

But it was never picked up on that at least one of us needed specialized counselling for traumatised children. Mother had another baby girl which she was allowed to keep, but Tony ended up in prison. Some said that she never allowed Dad to get cold in his grave before she decided to warm up her bed. The fact was that people might have had less to say about Mother's sexual behaviours on her quest for what she saw as love, had they done more than drink with my father. Maybe it might have been a far different ball game if some of these gossiping folk tried living with him.

I am unsure of the year my mother met her next intended but meet him she did. While Tony was doing his time, she sent him a Dear John and off she went with her new interest of moment. She started to visit us all and brought me a brand-new dress and cardigan, which happened to be two sizes too small. You see, I hadn't set eyes on Mum for a few years and her memory of me was obviously that I was much smaller than I was. She wanted me to go and visit her as she was doing all in her power with the social services to try and get us home again. They wanted her to begin slowly with us by visiting us all first, and if that went well, we could go home for afternoons and depending on how that went, maybe a day visit followed by a weekend. But I was not ready for a home visit yet, so I said no. I didn't feel comfortable with that at the minute. I couldn't forget the last experience I had gone through with her.

It was yet another time the Social Services had allowed her back into our lives and eventually doing everything she was trying to do now, they allowed us all back home to her. Within months it had all gone pear shaped again and she was back to her old ways. It ended with Mother being summoned to attend the children's family court again the next morning. There seemed a pattern with the Social Services and Mum, whereby we were in and out of care a few times.

On the one occasion I think Tony must have been in prison because I did not see him around. It was before the arrival of her second husband, but after the birth of her tenth child. My new baby sister was amazing - she was perfect and as cute as a button.

We weren't home more than a few months before Mother found it hard to cope again. She would never admit this, but it was obvious when her drinking got worse again. In me she had a housekeeper and child minder, not to say personal skivvy and general dogsbody. I wasn't afraid of her the way I was Dad, but she had a temper, and I felt the raff of that at times. I was obedient and respectful to her, which I had been taught form a young age in hospital, to be seen and not heard, to always behave like a young lady, and always respect my elders, which I did.

Mum went out more and more and again she left us to fend for ourselves. I hadn't been home very long, in-fact I was on a school holiday from my residential school. This was another humiliating time for me as she would never collect me from the rendezvous point where other parents collected their girls.

We all left school early on the final morning and got onto the coach heading for the meeting place in Birmingham where our parents had to come and collect us from the teachers. My Mother never ever picked me up, it was so embarrassing. I was always last to leave, and I was mortified seeing the teachers having to hang on until a welfare officer picked me up to take me home.

When I got home the place was filthy and impoverished as I had known it so often. I could hear my little twin brothers who were shouting and crying, so I went upstairs to the cot which both stood in naked, except for a dirty vest and from head to foot, cot and all, they were covered in shit. I was disgusted.

Here I was two minutes in the door, and I knew I would have to deal with this; I couldn't leave those two beautiful little boys like that. I felt they must have been freezing in just a vest and nothing more on. There was excrement all over the cot mattress, blanket, sides of the cot and all over the cot bars. The children were covered in it, including their little faces. There were chunks in the hair, their ears, nails, hands, and mouths - for it seemed they had even been eating their own faeces.

I felt sick but managed to take them one by one and clean them and their one cot. They kept putting their foul hands up for me to pick them up and hug them, but I had to be careful grabbing them from the back trying to keep the muck off myself. Most children have play flights where they sling cream pies at each other for fun. These too were a bit young to realize the full impact of their doings, but they knew it was poo-poo, stinky and dirty and decided to have a turd fight.

Another time I felt sickened and saddened, was when I noticed my little sister lying in her pram out-side the back door with no nappy on and she had messed herself. To my horror it looked like her crap was moving, but it was maggots or worms riddling about inside her waste. This was so shocking.

We endlessly had bed bugs, fleas, head lice and scabies. I was mortified every time we had to attend the scabies clinic and be bathed there and then a white lotion put all over us which burned us awfully. The children hated it and made such a fuss. They refused to have the lotion on and fought the nurse so they couldn't apply it. Never-the-less eventually they managed to apply the lotion and then had to suffer the younger ones screaming for 30 minutes until the burning eased.

Mum was never grateful regardless to what I did. She would scream and shout at me, pull me around the room by my hair and beat me over the head and back with a sweeping brush. Boy that hurt. She publicly humiliated me often, saying the most hurtful and spiteful things which chopped away awfully at my self-esteem.

I often wondered why she continued to send us for condoms. If it was supposed to be a family planning aid, it obviously wasn't working seeing that she was still having babies. I mean, she never brought condoms when Dad was alive so why buy them after he was gone, I often asked myself. I soon came to realize it was for when she left the pubs with these dirty old pervs.

Mother decided I was going back to the residential school, and I guess I was fine with that too at that point. I can't recall attending any school at this point of my life. I didn't even mind being her personal slave, but I did mind her lack of gratitude, constant ridicule, and endless outbursts of violence. I swore to myself if she was horrible to me again, I was not taking it. She didn't do it with the other children. They gave her dogs abuse and wouldn't tolerate her treating them like it. She would always try to get the siblings fighting as well; I thought that was just awful.

One day she started again when I was sweeping the floor. She grabbed my hair shouting at me. I remember pushing her against the wall and swinging the sweeping brush at her shouting, 'I will smash your head in with this if you touch me again.' She tried to get my sisters to jump on me, but I pinned them up the wall too.

I was so angry, she kept shouting, 'Stop her, Sally's gone crazy!' I hadn't gone crazy at all. I'd simply had enough of her nonsense. Regardless to how respectful and obedient I was to that woman, she treated me badly. It seems respectful behaviour was viewed as a weakness and in return she bullied me, and for the last time I felt I had enough of this woman and this life and as far as I was concerned. I was out of there, and so I ran off again to my Aunty Gwen.

This time she phoned the Social Services who allowed me to stay with her overnight after telling her to present me at family courts at 10 am the next morning. I told Aunty Gwen everything that was happening with us. I didn't mention the incest though because I was too embarrassed to go down that route and it seemed less painful to deal with if I tried to forget it.

The next morning Mother had to bring all the children to court and when I arrived, I looked so clean and well-dressed compared to the other siblings because Aunty Gwen had dressed me. Mum gave me some awful looks and had some awful digs at me.

'Why did you tell them about the condoms and why this, why that you little bastard? You've swore your father's life away and now you're swearing my life away you evil little bitch.'

I ignored her so she mocked me when no-one was around, 'Look at her Lady f***ing muck. You lot need to batter the head off her!'

The children loved me so weren't interested. For deep in their little hearts, they knew I loved them and cared, they knew I wouldn't harm them in anyway. The fact was, I wasn't trying to swear away my little siblings' life. I was trying to give them a chance and hopefully get them a life. They were born into this way of living and knew no other way, to them it was normal. I may have been born into this, but I was removed as a baby and brought-up so differently. I wanted them to know there was much more for them out there than they could ever imagine and even now it was possible for them to find that love they so deserved. It wasn't too late for us to find our stolen childhoods.

CHAPTER 31

By the time I was fourteen, I had been in the care system a few years and I was settled in a new school. Obviously, I was behind at school at first, but I didn't do too badly in our exams. I came first in the class in Religious Instruction, and sixth out of forty-six in maths; I loved history and art, singing and drama and did well in all of these, but I struggled with spelling and reading.

My adolescent years were a bit shaky I guess, due to the huge chip I carried on my shoulder. A lot of kids came from the care homes at my school, so it was pointless feeling sorry for myself for we all had a story to tell. My nick name at school was peg-leg due to my boots and callipers. I also wore round national health spectacles, and I looked a right nerd, so often got the micky took out of me. It was either Peg leg or Twiggy because of my big boobs.

One evening after tea I was playing outside my cottage home. Some of us kids from other cottages in the homes met up and hung about together. One of our friends, a lad called Peter who was about fifteen was playing with a knife. I was shocked and hated knifes so told him to get it away from us. He was telling me to shut up, but I persisted that he must put that knife away. I didn't want it in our company.

Peter could be a bit of a bully so not many stood up to him. We got into an argument that night and he told me to shut my mouth immediately or he would stab me. I told him he wouldn't dare, and he plunged the knife right through my arm and stabbed me. I was stunned, I couldn't believe it.

I ran in and told the house parents that I had fallen on a bottle. I had to be taken to hospital for stiches where I had about eight stiches in the wound and a couple around the other side of my arm where the tip of the blade had come out. He stabbed the knife straight through my arm you see. I never told on him, so he got away with it. It is only in later years that I realized letting him get away with that was indeed very foolish. Who knows what he could or has done to others over the years, for that was truly a behaviour which certainly needed to be addressed.

Another time I was exposed to violent behaviours by other youngsters was at school one day as I was entering my fifteenth year. I was having a row with big Tommy, another kid from the homes. Again, he was another bully who loved to throw his weight about. He was ordering me about and I wouldn't have it. I refused to do his bidding and even dismissed him at times which seriously wounded his pride.

It was almost the end of our lunch hour, and we were in our classroom ready for our teacher to enter. Tommy suddenly lost his temper and forcibly slung a big heavy book at my head. It knocked me over and as I fell; I smashed my head on the huge classroom pipes knocking myself spark out. I was told later; just as he threw the book the teacher entered our class and witnessed the event. But the next thing I can remember was waking up in casualty having a head x-ray and being diagnosed as having concussion, so I had to stay in all night. I never saw Tommy after that. I would imagine he was charged and taken off to a stricter home where the boys where locked in and monitored, a place for lads with behaviour problems who have issues adjusting to the natural run of things in care.

I started to write to one of my Irish Uncles on my mother's side. He was a really nice guy, and he sent the house parents my expenses so I could go to Dublin for a holiday, and so I did. I loved Dublin and had a wonderful time with my grandmother and Uncles. Yes, Granny did love her drink, but she was good to me and I really liked her. My youngest two Uncles were close to my age. In-fact there was only about sixteen months between Grandma having her youngest son and Mum having me. My Uncle was older but good company for me in Ireland and we had some great fun.

After a few weeks I refused to return to the home, so the Irish police or Social Services went to my uncle's work, seeing that he was the adult who was accountable for me and demanded that he return me to Birmingham care system immediately. When he came to my grandmothers that afternoon, he was not a happy bunny and demanded that I was taken to the boat and returned the following morning and so I was.

When I returned, I was sent straight from the care home I'd been in for a few years to a care hostel because I had now left school. I hated it there. The girls were strangers, selfish and older than me. I couldn't get on with the house parents particularly the house Mother. Wow she was moody, nasty, and verbally aggressive. She screamed and shouted a lot when the Social Services weren't around, and if she couldn't take to a girl, she never made our life easy. I tried to make it work but hated it there, so I ran off. In fact, I ran off a lot.

This one time I was almost sixteen and sick and tired of being in care. I hadn't seen my brothers and sisters for years and sadly they were fading to the back of my mind. I could never understand why we had to call house parents Mum and Dad, it just did not feel right, then the other staff aunty, it seemed so false, more so as we couldn't stand them half of the time. I ran and ran and had to go back time and time again, and the house Mother always took it personally.

The last time I ran away, on my return I was forced to go to the VD clinic. I was really scared and did not understand what this was. I asked if someone could come with me, but I was told if I was big enough to run off, then I was big enough to go to the VD hospital alone and get a test. I went and when I got there, I was asked a lot of personal questions which only added to my awkwardness and sheer discomfort. Here I was at just almost sixteen; actually fifteen, alone in this horrid place surrounded by all sorts of people. Today I realize that many where prostitutes and drug addicts.

I was taken into the Doctor who with a nurse got me to remove my bottom clothing. I got tearful saying I didn't want to but the Social Services wanted this, so it seemed it had to be done, or woe-be-tide us when we got back to the hostel. I was trembling as they took swabs from my throat and other parts of my body. Not only was this terribly embarrassing for me I felt so humiliated and disgusted that they were doing these things I did not understand, and they really hurt me as they prodded about.

'Relax,' the nurse would say, but how could I? Tears rolled down my face as I lay silently weeping and I bit my hand trying to put up with it. I felt helpless to stop them and violated all over again. Here was somebody doing what they wanted to the personal parts of my body again and I was powerless to stop them. There was no way I could relax and being so tensed up it obviously hurt a lot more. I was so sore when it was all over, and I was dismissed to get dressed and wait in the waiting room. I felt this was so unfair. This had been a huge ordeal for me, and it seemed, nobody cared or was prepared to help me through it all.

Shame on the Social Service I felt and some of these house mothers. I couldn't help but wonder, did they know the true history of many of these kids in their care or where they just believing what was on their case book files? After a while I was called back into the Doctor again. I was asked to sit down, and the Doctor started to inform me that I had gonorrhoea. I had to ask him what that was, and almost died of shame when he told me. The Doctor went on to ask me what the name of the man I had slept with was, so they could inform him that he must come to the clinic and get some treatment.

'I don't have a man,' I said. 'There is no one.'

They continued to ask and coax me to tell them who this man was, but I couldn't for there wasn't one, which they wouldn't believe. I silently wept all the way home, only to be greeted by the house mother who sat me down for hours trying to demand the name of this so-called guy I had slept with. She got no-where so I was allowed to go to bed as I was drained. On my way to my room, I went to the loo with an ach in my private parts. As I sat down and began to wee-wee, I felt the most awful sting and some very bright blood burst out of me. Then the bleeding stopped.

The next day a Social Worker arrived and persisted to ask me for ages who had I slept with. 'Nobody,' I continued to reply.

'There must somebody,' they persisted to say.
We were getting no-where and I was feeling intimidated between the Social Worker and this unkind uncaring bossy bullying house mother. So, I agreed and gave them a man's name I knew and an address to find him. He was not pleased when I next saw him neither was his lady, for he had done nothing to deserve what I said but was kind enough to understand why I did it. I was being interrogated so much I simply said anything to get them to back off and leave me be.

The truth was, the only person who had been at me in a sexual way, was my father. This being the case, I must have caught this filthy disease from him and furthermore and even harder for me to think about, was the fact I had got this scummy vile thing inside me and now I knew it had been there for years. Nobody in any of the homes or the social service ever got on to that.

For six weeks I had to go to that awful degrading place for a jab in the arse and by the end of it I had truly had enough. Regardless to how much I scrubbed I could never feel clean. That whole matter blew my mind and was a very deep secret most of my life.

I had not been in contact with my siblings for a good while now, but I knew they were safe and well cared for in their different care homes. I started a job in an office as a filing Clark and hated it. I found it so boring so didn't stick it out for long.

I was determined to not make the same mistakes as my mother. I realized if my life was to change, then only I could change it and this I was more than sure I was going to do. I had Ireland in my blood, and so one night when all were asleep, I sneaked down the stairs at the girls' hostel opened the window putting my case out, and then climbed out and quietly ran over to my friend's car who was waiting to pick me up.

As I looked back, I knew I would never go back there again, and I didn't. The next evening, I stepped of the boat in Dublin and couldn't help but think - what a coincidence! Here was I doing exactly the same thing as my mother, only she stood in England and boarded her train to Birmingham, while I stood in Dunlerry boarding mine for Dublin - only now it was 35 years later. There I was at sweet sixteen feeling as free as a bird and a million dollars, as I thought *the world is your oyster, Sally.*

I picked up my shabby brown case as I took a deep breath and cheerfully skipped down the road humming towards my grandmothers. Little did I know that this road to freedom was actually a road to ruin, and the trials that I had faced up to at this point - seemed to fade away in comparison to the nightmares that were to haunt me. The road to Dublin was about to lead me on to the road to nowhere. What I thought would give me freedom was going to bring me bondage and degradation. I had yet one of the greatest battles of a person's life to face, as I stood in my dungeon of cast iron bars searching for my road to freedom, my escape route from life its very self and the only place I couldn't get out of - the prison within myself.

Printed in Great Britain
by Amazon

37720524R00150